# ME NOR CA

Travel with Marco Polo
Insider Tips

**INSIDER TIP**
Your shortcut
to a great
experience

# MARCO POLO
# TOP HIGHLIGHTS

## PORT CRUISE IN MAÓ ⭐
Explore Menorca's capital from the water; it's on one of the world's longest bays.
📷 *Tip: Take an early-morning boat to catch the first rays of sun bathing the bay in wonderful light.*

➤ p. 50, Maó & the Eastern Tip

## MONTE TORO ⭐
From Menorca's highest peak, don't miss the fabulous view over hills, gorges and the coast.
📷 *Tip: For the best photos, get there early, before the heat haze descends over the landscape.*

➤ p. 75, Tramuntana & the North

## CAMÍ DE CAVALLS ⭐
Walk the island's coastal path – even the shortest stretches are enchanting!

➤ p. 36, Sport & activities

## CALA MITJANA ⭐
This little bay is a piece of paradise, framed by pines and beautiful cliffs.

➤ p. 85, Migjorn, the Centre & the South

## CIUTADELLA ⭐
Mediterranean living in the island's prettiest town, with its romantic port, narrow streets and Moorish palaces.
📷 *Tip: The pretty cobbled streets are best photographed in the glow of their streetlights.*

➤ p. 94, Ciutadella & the Western Tip

## BOAT TRIPS FROM CIUTADELLA ⭐
Chug along the southern coast to see Menorca's finest beaches and emerald waters – take full advantage of the chance to jump in!

➤ p. 101, Ciutadella & the Western Tip

### CALA MACARELLA ⭐7
No wonder images of this bay are used to publicise the island! Its waters are a turquoise treasure.

➤ p. 105, Ciutadella & the Western Tip

### CAP DE FAVÀRITX ⭐8
If you get bored of Menorca's white sands, the rugged dark slate on this cape provides a perfect contrast (photo).
📷 *Tip: The slate's crystals glimmer in the light of the rising sun – when it is also gloriously empty here.*

➤ p. 72, Tramuntana & the North

### CAP DE CAVALLERIA ⭐9
This lighthouse sits alone on tall cliffs; the northernmost point on the Balearics is one of Menorca's wildest spots.
📷 *Tip: White walls, blue seas and skies – a perfect evening photo, especially when a boat chugs past.*

➤ p. 70, Tramuntana & the North

### S'ALBUFERA DES GRAU ⭐10
Beautiful lagoons with forests and fields, marshes and lakes.

➤ p. 72, Tramuntana & the North

# CONTENTS

CIUTADELLA & THE WESTERN TIP

TRAMUNTANA & THE NORTH

MIGJORN, CENTRE & THE SOUTH

MAÓ & THE EASTERN TIP

# CONTENTS

---

| | | | |
|---|---|---|---|
| ⊙ Plan your visit | ⍥ Eating/drinking | | 🦩 Rainy day activities |
| €–€€€ Price categories | 👜 Shopping | | 🐷 Budget activities |
| (*) Premium-rate phone number | ⍫ Going out | | 😎 Family activities |
| | 🌴 Top beaches | | ⚑ Classic experiences |

(*A2*) Refers to the removable pull-out map
(0) Located off the map

Ciutadella de Menorca

# BEST OF
# MENORCA

Cala Macarella is one of the most beautiful coves on the island

# BEST ☂ WHEN IT RAINS

## ACTIVITIES TO BRIGHTEN YOUR DAY

### HISTORY & MYTHS

A portal to the past: the *Museu de Menorca* in an old monastery in Maó has exhibits on all aspects of Menorcan history, from ancient crafts to contemporary art.

➤ p. 46, Maó & the Eastern Tip

### OPULENT OPERA

Amazingly, this small island is home to Spain's oldest opera house, built in 1829. High art decorates Maó's *Teatre* auditorium and a grand chandelier hangs from its domed ceiling. The space is so intimate that you can almost touch the performers. A variety of music is performed all year round, except in November when it is reserved for opera.

➤ p. 52, Maó & the Eastern Tip

### CANNON FIRE

Thundering cannons, a sea of flags and the heat of battle. Experience the historical siege of the island – thankfully it's only virtual – at the massive, British-built *Fort Marlborough* near Es Castell.

➤ p. 57, Maó & the Eastern Tip

### SOUVENIR SHOPPING

From the beautiful to the bizarre: craftspeople sell their wares at the *Centre Artesanal de Menorca* in Es Mercadel. Visitors can watch the crafters at work and explore the island's craft heritage at the on-site museum. If a special something catches your eye, snap it up before it goes.

➤ p. 74, Tramuntana & the North

### A GIFT FROM GOD

Gothic glory in Ciutadella's *Catedral*: huge columns, filigree windows and expressive sculptures adorn this house of God … and there's a treasury too (photo).

➤ p. 94, Ciutadella & the Western Tip

# BEST ON A BUDGET

## FOR SMALLER WALLETS

### A VIEW WORTHY OF A KING
The island's main environmental organisation *(GOB Menorca)* has its base in the capital at the *Molí del Rei* ("King's Mill"), which has splendid views of Maó's town and harbour. Admission is free.
➤ p. 47, Maó & the Eastern Tip

### ARCHAIC ARCHITECTURE
If you want to explore Menorca's pre-history, the *Talaiot de Trepucó* is one of the island's best sites; it's thousands of years old and admission is free.
➤ p.53, Maó & the Eastern Tip

### GREEN LAGOON
You can visit the protected wetlands *S'Albufera d'es Grau* – with their rich variety of flora and fauna – on your own or as part of a free group tour. They are spectacular between April and June when the flowers are in bloom. There are beaches too (photo).
➤ p. 73, Tramuntana & the North

### TAKE THE BUS TO THE BEACH
In the summer months, *Cala Macarella*, a stunning beach in a conservation area, is only accessible by bus. This means no negotiating long traffic jams or packed car parks. The bus is cheap and departs from Ciutadella – a great, green way to start a day at the beach!
➤ p. 105, Ciutadella & the Western Tip

### FREE OPEN-AIR OBSERVATORY
Some places on the north coast are so free of light pollution that you can see thousands of stars with the naked eye. One of the best places for this is *Punta Nati* on the northwestern tip of the island.
➤ p. 106, Ciutadella & the Western Tip

# BEST WITH CHILDREN

## FUN FOR YOUNG AND OLD

### ANIMAL MAGIC

*Es Lloc de Menorca* is an excellent zoo whose prime focus is conservation. Children can hold birds of prey on their arms, walk around enclosures, stroke Madagascan lemurs and feed farm animals. Sound good? It is just east of Alaior.

➤ p. 81, Migjorn, Centre & the South

### GEOLOGICAL GENIUSES

Do your kids love learning? The *Centre de Geología de Menorca* in Ferreries will teach them why the rocks on Menorca have such distinctive colours.

➤ p. 82, Migjorn, Centre & the South

### THOROUGH THOROUGHBREDS

"Dancing and dreaming" is how they describe the horses that prance and pirouette in *Somni*, an equestrian show on the *Son Martorellet* estate. A visit to the stables to watch them practise is perhaps even better than the show itself. The *finca* is surrounded by pines and olive groves near Ferreries.

➤ p. 83, Migjorn, Centre & the South

### SURFING, SNORKELLING, SAILING

There are water-sports centres in every resort on the island offering plenty for kids to do, from windsurfing to bouncing around on a banana boat. *Surf & Sail* in Son Xoriguer comes particularly highly recommended.

➤ p. 103, Ciutadella & the Western Tip

### WATER LOT OF FUN

Menorca's biggest water park, *Aqua Center*, boasts long slides, an "adventure river", a "black hole", jacuzzies, bouncy castles and a go-karting course.

➤ p. 107, Ciutadella & the Western Tip

# BEST ⚑

## CLASSIC EXPERIENCES

**ONLY ON MENORCA**

### DISAPPEARING FORTRESSES

Most fortresses on the island were constructed in the era of piracy and the colonial wars. Nature has reclaimed many of the buildings but some of them have been preserved, such as the fortress of *La Mola* and the *Castell de Sant Felip* near Maó.
➤ p. 53 & p. 57, Maó & the Eastern Tip

### LOBSTER STEW

It's not cheap, but the original *caldereta* – preferably served in an earthenware *olla* – should be tasted as part of any trip to Menorca. It's best eaten in places near the sea, such as the pretty village of Fornells in the north.
➤ p. 68, Tramuntana & the North

### GORGES TO THE SEA

Typical for Menorca's sunny south side are the gorges that run out into small coves with white sands against a backdrop of the azure sea. A good example is *Cala Trebalúger* near Cala Mitjana.
➤ p. 85, Migjorn, Centre & the South

### IN SEARCH OF EVERYDAY CUISINE

Erected in the middle of the 19th century and recently renovated, the *Mercat* (market) in Ciutadella, with its green and white tiles, has a timeless quality. Here you can watch locals as they go about their shopping and try plenty of local specialities.
➤ p. 98, Ciutadella & the Western Tip

### ON HORSEBACK

Horses are to Menorca what kangaroos are to Australia. Get close to the beautiful creatures by booking a trail ride (photo) with, for example, the *Cavalls Son Àngel* estate – or attend celebrations sucha as *Festes de la Verge de Gràcia* in Maó
➤ p. 109, Ciutadella & the Western Tip, p. 127, Festivals & events

---

# GET TO KNOW MENORCA

Time passes slowly under the palm trees of the Plaça de Alfons III in Ciutadella

# DISCOVER MENORCA

Peace and quiet now reign at La Mola fortress, which guards Maó's harbour

Wherever you look there are beautiful beaches with the azure sea blending into the bright blues skies above, rock formations in pastel colours, fragrant pine forests and hilly pastures. Maybe the landscape is the reason why the islanders here are so relaxed and laid-back.

## RELAXED LIVING

On Menorca, you'll often hear the phrase *a poc a poc*, which means "slowly, slowly". The islanders like to take time for the good things in life: for friends and family, good food and drink, enjoying the natural world and simply day-dreaming. Driving, ordering in a restaurant, shopping – everything is done at a leisurely pace.

The Menorcans have created small oases of relaxation within their towns and even the most mundane street is perked up by a bar where people meet to

**c. 2800 BCE**
First settlers arrive from today's France and Spain

**1500 BCE**
*Talaiot* culture: walled towns and sacred buildings

**From 123 BCE**
Roman occupation

**CE 903–1287**
Arabic occupation; Menorca is part of the Cordoba Caliphate

**1287**
Reconquista: Alfonso III of Aragon conquers Menorca

**1712**
Great Britain occupies Menorca

**1782**
Spain conquers the island

gossip over a *pomada* (gin with lemonade). The Menorcan lifestyle also includes a refreshing dip in the sea – best repeated daily. And you won't need to travel far to swim, as there's a beautiful bay waiting right around every corner. That's why Menorca is rightly considered sweeter and quieter than the other Balearic Islands. It's further from the Spanish mainland and was developed later than Mallorca, which helped it avoid many of the effects of mass tourism, like ugly hotels or drunken revellers. Visitors to Menorca love the idyllic bays, romantic old towns and mysterious relics from the distant past.

## THE CRAGGY NORTH WITH ITS CLIFFS & FJORDS

Although the island is relatively small, there's a vast difference between the north and south. Tramuntana in the north is characterised by deep rocky fjords which cut a long way inland. The landscape is dominated by dark rock, which, shaped by wind and sea, gives the coastline a rugged edge. The area has always been more scarcely populated than the centre and the south coast. There are numerous island legends attached to sites along the windswept northern coast. The landscape in the northwest is dominated by pastureland. Golden cornfields and wildflowers turn this area into a riot of colour in spring and autumn. The vegetation often extends right down to the coast, clinging ever more tightly to the rocky soil. Only the outermost tips of land, the capes, are completely barren. Here, on stormy days in the autumn or spring, sea spray showers the dark coastal cliffs with a white deposit of salt.

**1798**
The Brits return

**1802**
Menorca becomes a permanent part of Spain

**1936–39**
General Franco wins the Spanish Civil War and Spain becomes a dictatorship until 1975

**1983**
The Balearic Islands receive devolved powers

**1993**
The island is declared a biosphere reserve

**Spring 2021**
Low Covid-19 rates mean the first tourists return to the island

## THE MILD SOUTH WITH ITS MANY BEACHES

Migjorn in the south is completely different, with a more sheltered coastline made up of small bays, wooded valleys and gorges. The southern part of Menorca consists of a 50–60-m-high limestone plateau which gently slopes to the south and is only interrupted by the course of drainage channels or *barrancs*. This is the sunny side of Menorca, where the architecture is more delicate and pine trees rise up to the sky. It's largely sheltered from the strong winds that (mostly in winter) sweep across the north of the island at speeds of more than 100kmh. Most of the beaches are situated in the south, which is why most tourists are drawn there.

The east and west of the island are as different as the north and south coast. In the east is industrious, British-influenced Maó, and in the west the more rebellious and permissive Spanish Ciutadella. Competition between the cities began with the British occupation. In the early 18th century, the Brits relocated the capital city from Ciutadella to Maó because Maó had a better natural harbour. For Ciutadella, this meant that the local nobility and clergy were abruptly removed from their dominance over the island. And even today, Ciutadella natives tend to avoid Maó.

## A LONG WAY BACK

People are believed to have lived on Menorca for more than 6,500 years, the first settlers probably having come across the sea on reed boats. Some rock wall drawings in Menorca's caves depict boats which are very similar to illustrations found on Crete. The oldest stone constructions are up to 4,000 years old. Later, Phoenicians, Greeks, Carthaginians and Romans used the island's strategic location, while the Byzantines and finally the Arabs subjugated it.

## LOOKING FORWARD

Today, around 60 per cent of all the islanders are employed in tourism. However, the island's government is trying to promote a gentler kind of travel, and understands the *Reserva de la Biosfera* designation not just as a marketing ploy but as a clarion call to use tourism to maintain a largely unspoiled island. Their motto on this is: *Ets Menorca, no frissis!* – You're on Menorca, so take your time!

Although, like everywhere else, Menorca was hit by the coronavirus pandemic, the island emerged relatively unscathed. The Balearics, along with the Canary Islands, were some of the least-affected provinces in Spain. However, the pandemic did have an impact – for three months in 2020, Menorcans were subjected to Spain's emergency laws. This extreme lockdown meant soldiers patrolling the streets – something that had not happened since 1936 during the Spanish Civil War.

# AT A GLANCE

**93,400**
**Population**

Isle of Wight: 143,000

**1,000**
Archaeological sites

The most in the Balearics

**216km**
**Length of coastline**

Sussex coastline: 220km

**697km²**
**Area**

Isle of Skye: 1,656km²

**HIGHEST MOUNTAIN:**
**MONTE TORO**
**357m**

Mount Teide on
Tenerife: 3,718m

**LONG-DISTANCE PATH**
**125km**
is the length of the
Camí de Cavalls, or
"horse path"

**MOST POPULAR**
**MONTH TO TRAVEL**

**JULY**

## 1.5 MILLION HOLIDAYMAKERS
visit Menorca every year, of whom 0.5 million are Brits
Mallorca: 11 million tourists per year, of whom 4.5 million are German

# CIUTADELLA
Largest city, with 30,600 inhabitants
Maó has 29,500 inhabitants

**400 SPERM WHALES**
live in the sea around the
Balearics

**4000** Menorquí horses
live on the island

# UNDERSTAND MENORCA

## BIRDWATCHING

Don't forget your earplugs if you hike to Punta S'Escullar! The chirping, twittering and screeching that you'll often encounter here is so deafening that it drowns out the sound of the waves crashing into the northern cliffs. Flocks of Scopoli's shearwater fly overhead. These seabirds are related to the albatross and a whopping one million mating pairs live on the desolate cliffs located a 30-minute walk west of Cala Morell. It's the largest colony in this part of the Mediterranean. Incidentally, Scopoli's shearwaters don't like to be approached, and they will take revenge by emptying their bowels on the nearest target …

The fact that birds feel so at home on Menorca is due to its ideal location between Europe and Africa. Some feathered creatures enjoy Menorca so much that they never want to leave – including the kingfisher, which is easily identified by its bright blue and orange feathers, as well as the black-and-white-striped and "mohawked" Eurasian hoopoe and the white-headed red kite. If you see a white body with dark-edged wings flying high above you, it's probably a black vulture (*alimoche* in Spanish), which has also settled here and has even become Menorca's mascot. The best areas for birdwatching are the S'Albufera des Grau marshes on the east coast and Prat de Son Bou on the southern coast – you can join guided birdwatching tours there *(menorcawalkingbirds.com)*.

## BINI WHAT?

Pretty soon, your head will be swimming with all the place names that start with "Bini": Binibèquer, Binifancolla, Biniarocca, Binillautí... But what on earth does this prefix mean? Arabic speakers will know immediately: *Bini* means "property of the sons of…" and implies that the places once belonged to the sons of Bèquer, Fancolla, Rocca and Llautí. The prefix "Al" also appears frequently, in names such as Alaior. These geographical designations are also a legacy of the Arabs who conquered the Balearic Islands in CE 903 after taking the Iberian mainland. They were tolerant towards those of other faiths, and Christians and Jews were allowed to practise their religion. The Christian conquerors, on the other hand, spoke a very different language: one of violence and military might. When King Alfonso III of Aragón captured the Balearic Islands in 1287, the Arabs were enslaved, their property looted, their mosques razed. In fact, the Ciutadella cathedral was once an enormous Muslim house of worship – but it's barely recognisable as such today.

## COOL

"Better in winter" is the slogan Menorca is using to attract new visitors. And it's the truth! It might be somewhat inconvenient to get to

Visit in winter to enjoy the beach all to yourself

Menorca in the cooler months (October to mid-May), but the low season offers a number of advantages. The meadows burst into bloom with the first autumn rains, creating pastures where cows suddenly emerge from their shady summer stalls to graze. The Menorcans refer to this phenomenon as "our autumn-spring". The restaurants that are still open during this season are mainly frequented by locals; traditional holidays are celebrated, and the locals hold sporting events for which the summer weather would be too hot. The off season is also much nicer for hiking or cycling. The one problem is that many hotels in popular resorts are closed, but you can always stay in Ciutadella or Maó.

## ARCHITECTURAL EYESORES

Since the 1960s, the neighbouring island of Mallorca has paved over one stretch of coastline after the next. The founding of a "Group to Protect Birds and Nature" (gobmenorca.com) in 1971 was a first humble attempt at stopping the destruction of the Balearic Islands. It wasn't until 20 years later that a nature conservation law went into effect – and it was fiercely enforced on Menorca. A whopping 43 per cent of the island's land was protected by the nature conservation law (the European average is just 7 per cent!), and building on the coast is prohibited, with the exception of the territory of Ciutadella and south of Maó. The northern half of

Menorca (Tramuntana) is also closed to construction projects, as are large swaths of the island's inland regions. And in 1993, conservation efforts

Cala Galdana

were rewarded once again: Menorca was named a UNESCO Biosphere Reserve *(biosferamenorca.org)*. It might sound like a marketing tactic, a sort of meaningless banner that the Menorcans proudly display to attract tourists, but no, it's a process, and every year, they have to prove that they aren't sacrificing environmental protection on the altar of economic development. In order to lend weight to these claims, Menorca's

municipalities have also committed to upholding the UN Agenda Local 21, which states that the economy is geared toward sustainable development so that future generations will also be able to enjoy Menorca's nature.

## BEWARE OF THE BRITS

Menorca is the British island. And it's no wonder: Great Britain ruled Menorca for 71 years. The British occupied it three times, for increasingly shorter time periods: first from 1706 to 1754, then from 1763 to 1782, then finally from 1798 to 1802, when they returned it to Spain for good.

And what remains of this colonial heritage? The black-and-white Friesian cows that the British brought to produce large quantities of high-fat milk to make good cheese are one obvious remnant, but British-style gin is also ubiquitous, in fact it has become Menorca's national drink. British sailors and soldiers taught the Menorcans how to distil it from purified alcohol and juniper. And you will run into many English words that have been so corrupted over time that it's almost impossible to recognise them: For example, you can close the *vindou* (window), eat *bifi* (beef) for lunch, or have a quick drink – *ha fet un trinqui*, which will make you feel *lesi* (lazy).

The massive *Fort Marlborough* near Maó, with its cannons and casemates, is also part of the British legacy. Nearby is Georgetown (today known as Es Castell), a garrison city with a military base attached, and roads arranged in a grid. The British are additionally responsible for the first road connecting east and west, which they constructed in 1722 and which is still named after Governor Richard Kane *(Camí d'en Kane)* today. Incidentally, Kane isn't viewed as an evil occupier, but rather as a liberator from a backward feudal system.

## PREHISTORIC STRUCTURES

Relics of a prehistoric age might at first conjure up boring lessons at school but on Menorca this dry history comes alive with gruesome stone sacrificial tables and much else besides! *Talaiot* (2500–123 BCE) is the name used to describe the society that existed on Menorca during the Iron Age. It erected impressive megaliths and, although these monuments can be found on the other Balearic islands, Menorca has the most with a total of 1,600 sites of which 274 contain well-preserved ruins.

The sites are spread across the island with the majority found in the island's fertile south. The word *talaiot* originates from the Arabic word *atalaya* (lookout tower) and indeed most of the monuments are situated on mounds. There are three types of constructions: *talaiots* ("lookout towers"), *taules* ("tables") and *navetas* ("ships") shaped like the hull of an upturned ship. It is presumed that these were used as graves. *Talaiots* are round or rectangular-shaped structures made of large stones without the use of mortar. The *taules* can be up to 3m in height and consist of vertical pillars with a horizontal stone lying on them. Although their exact significance is unknown, one theory is they

were where Celtic Druids performed human sacrifices. It is more likely, however, that the *taules* themselves represented a deity, for example a bull. The central stone T is almost always surrounded by a circle of monoliths. The whole complex, where a fire constantly burned and animal sacrifices were made, was for ritual purposes.

## TRUE OR FALSE?

### MENORCANS ARE NOT REALLY SPANIARDS

True! Islanders here are proud to be different to mainland Spain. They see themselves as more relaxed, less aggressive. Even their language – Menorquí – is much less staccato than Castilian Spanish. They think of themselves as closer to Barcelona's Catalans. And when Real Madrid meets Barcelona at football, there is never any doubt who Menorcans will back.

### MENORCANS ARE OBSESSED WITH HORSES

True! Menorca and horses belong together like bread and butter. There are prancing ponies at every festival as well as a "Horse Path" *(Camí de Cavalls)* and a Rider's Cape *(Cap de Cavalleria)* The island even has an endemic breed, the *Caballo Menorquín*, which is honoured every year in a special show, where the finest specimens on the island are selected.

## GORGEOUS GORGES

At just 357m, the largest mountain on Menorca is not exactly massive. And so, you wouldn't expect the island to have particularly diverse landscapes. But it does, thanks to the *barrancs* – *barrancos* in Spanish – or gullies created by running water, cut into the soft limestone by millennia of rain. There are 36 of them in the south of the island, stretching for kilometres along the coast and creating fantastic beaches at their estuaries and deltas.

The confluence of two *barrancs* in Son Bou is particularly beautiful where dunes and wetlands have formed. The *Barranc de Binigaus* – a deep green thicket with enormous caves – is also stunning. And in the *Barranc d'Algendar*, which winds from Ferreries to Cala Galdana, there's a forest of pines and cork oaks, making it a perfect place for hiking. The fact that the *barrancs* are usually lush and green is due to more than just the water that collects during rainfall; the canyon walls, which reach heights of up to 40m, also protect the gullies from the cold Tramuntana wind, creating a mild microclimate. The first French and Spanish settlers came to live in the southern *barrancs* – they knew where the living was good!

## NOT A WORD

The islanders generally understand Spanish but aren't too keen on speaking it. You may find that if you ask a question in Spanish, you'll receive an answer in *Menorquí*, and then you'll probably understand *nada* – nothing at all. If this happens, you might find English a bit more helpful. *Menorquí*, the Menorcan dialect, is one of the oldest dialects of *Català*, or Catalan, still in use today. Catalan was brought over from Aragón by King Alfonso III in 1287 and *Català* has been recognised since 1983 as an official language on the Balearics alongside Spanish. After the years of suppression of regional languages under Franco it now enjoys great popularity amongst the younger generation. Place names on road signs are now almost always in Catalan. *Català* is spoken in schools and at the University of the Balearic Islands, books are written in or translated into Catalan. And as many Catalans would like to break away from Spain, it's likely that the Spanish language will continue to be pushed further into the background as time goes on.

## STONE BY STONE

A wall nearly as long as the Great Wall of China? You can find it on the little island of Menorca! If you peer out of the window as your plane is landing, the landscape will look like a puzzle. And once you're on the island, you'll realise that the puzzle pieces are fields *(tanques)* separated from one another by walls *(parets)* 1-1.50m high. For centuries, the farmers of Menorca took upon themselves the Sisyphean task of building these drystone walls. The combined length of all the walls of Menorca is an astounding 20,000km, just 1,000km shorter than the Great Wall of China.

And what are the walls for? Simple: the farmers wanted to get the stones off the fields to make them easier to cultivate, and the walls protected plants from the wind and created enclosures for their precious livestock.

## MAYO FROM MAÓ

Everyone knows egg mayo. But where does its essential condiment come from originally? The proof that this white sauce originated on Menorca isn't yet 100% definitive, but there are many signs that point to the French Duke of Richelieu. During the brief period that France ruled the island (seven years in the mid-18th century), it's said that Richelieu helped mayonnaise achieve global fame. The Frenchman did more than just steal the heart of a woman from Maó (Spanish: *mahonesa*); he also picked up an important recipe from her: olive oil mixed with egg, a pinch of salt, and crushed garlic. It's very possible that this Balearic *alli oli* (garlic with oil) became its elegant, garlic-free French cousin, and that the *mahonesa*'s sauce became mayonnaise.

Delicate crocuses, cultivated for saffron, are well-protected by a traditional stone wall

# EATING
# SHOPPING
# SPORT

The glass-clear water at Arenal d'en Castell is perfect for snorkelling

# EATING & DRINKING

*Bon profit!* **Even if the prices of some *caldereta* suggest the opposite, this enthusiastic greeting is not uttered for the landlord's benefit, rubbing his hands eagerly as he presents you with the bill, but simply means "enjoy your meal".**

Menorcan cuisine is simple but hearty – proof that more calories mean more flavour. Historically opposed cultures are brought together on the plate: Arabic and Catalan recipes are adapted with a hint of Britishness or a *soupçon de française*.

### REGIONAL NOT INTERNATIONAL

Much of the food is produced locally, including vegetables such as tomatoes, artichokes, peas, beans, onions, potatoes, carrots and cabbage. And there is game, lamb, veal, pork and lots of fresh seafood – ideally served with garlic, olive oil and the island's aromatic herbs such as rosemary and thyme.

There is, of course, plenty of "international" cuisine here too, although the restaurants that serve it are mostly little more than tourist traps, closing as soon as the season ends and dishing up meagre portions of questionable meat (and occasionally) fish alongside huge plates of chips and salad. Try it if you feel the need but you will quickly be back eating from the island's *greixoneres* and *olles* (clay bowls and pots).

### CALDERETA – THE ICING ON THE CAKE OF MENORCAN CUISINE

Any of the posher menus on Menorca will include *caldereta* – lobster cooked in a delicate vegetable broth (the basic recipe is: onion, two cloves of garlic, tomato, leek, seasoned with two tablespoons of brandy and a sprig of parsley). A portion will cost about 80

---

Typical Menorcan fare: *Queso El Mahón*, salami and *ensaïmadas*

euros, but for this rather steep price tag you are invited to select your own live lobster, which is then transformed into something truly special.

## SWEET & SPICY PASTRIES

As soon as you arrive at the airport you will encounter stacks of *ensaïmadas*, a delicious, light, spiral-shaped pastry. It comes in various sizes and with different fillings, such as *cabello de ángel* (pumpkin jam), *crema* (custard) and *nata* (whipped cream), and is sold by almost all the bakeries on the island. It has to be made using pork lard (from which it derives its name – *saïm* means lard). *Crespells*, are equally sweet and sprinkled with icing sugar but are quite dry and crumble easily. They are made from a firm dough, as are *rubiolls*, which are then rolled out and can be filled with pumpkin jam or custard. Finally there are the *bunyols*, mainly available in the autumn, which

are whorls (similar to small, hand-made doughnuts) made from a semi-liquid dough of wheat or potato flour fried in hot oil. *Empanadas*, turn-overs filled with vegetables, pork, lamb or a meat-vegetable mix, are hearty and tasty.

## DID SOMEONE SAY SALAMI?

The best of the island's cold cuts is the *sobrasada*, a cured pork sausage which acquires its characteristic red colour from paprika. It is often sliced and fried and even combined with honey or *ensaïmadas*. *Butifarrones* (black pudding) and *carn i xulla* (comparable to a coarse pepper salami) are also available everywhere.

## CHEESY MOMENTS

Despite winning more than once at the World Cheese Awards, *Queso El Mahón* ("Maó Cheese" – its name refers to where it is shipped from) is

Need a quick pick me-up? It looks like water, but it's gin

"young" *(tierno)* which is buttery and sweet, to "semi-mature" *(semicurado)* which is nuttier, and mature *(curado)* which is tangier.

## TASTY BOTANICALS

The British may have brought gin to Menorca but the locals have very much adopted it as their favourite tipple. A distillery in Port de Maó produces gin in the traditional way while a younger generation has begun experimenting with botanicals typical to the island such as thyme and pine which feature in the wonderfully fruity Gin Glop. A popular and refreshing island cocktail is *pellofa*, gin with a generous splash of soda water and a slice of lemon. Copious amounts of *pomada*, a mix of gin and lemonade, are consumed, especially on feast days. *Herbes* (Spanish *hierbas*, or "herbs") originally comes from Ibiza, further to the west, but Menorca also has some outstanding examples of this sweet, yellow herbal liqueur. The two regional specialities are the typical Menorcan chamomile liqueur as well as *palo*, a liqueur made from the fruits of the carob tree.

**INSIDER TIP**
**Taste the forest**

little known outside Spain. It has a lightly tangy and robust flavour thanks to the lush Menorcan grass the cows feed on. The grass gets its water from rain which sweeps across the island on the Tramuntana wind – and it gets a delicious pinch of seasoning from the sea air. In order to provide more balance to the cheese, *Mahón* often contains up to 5% sheep's milk. There are different levels of maturity from

## Today's Specials

### Starters

**OLI I AIGUA**
A tomato soup packed with other vegetables and served in a clay bowl with thin slices of bread

**PILOTES**
Meatballs in an almond sauce

**COCA DE VERDURA**
Pizza-like pastries topped with vegetables

**ALBERGÍNIES AL FORN**
Aubergines stuffed with bread, eggs and herbs

### Main courses

**CALAMAR FARCIT**
Braised squid with a stuffing made from parsley, garlic, eggs and pine kernels

**PEIX EN ES FORN**
Oven-baked perch with potatoes, raisins, pine kernels, spinach and tomatoes

**CONILL AMB CEBES**
Rabbit stew with onions, langoustines and other seafood served in a clay bowl

**LLOM AMB COL**
Meat and cabbage stew with white wine, bacon, tomatoes, onions and garlic and served in a clay pot

### Desserts

**GREIXONERA DE BROSSAT**
Cream cheese baked in a clay pot with lemon and cinnamon

**FIGUES AL FORN**
Oven-roasted figs

**LLET FRITA**
Deep-fried, battered custard

### Drinks

**PELLOFA**
Gin and lemonade, served with lemon zest

**PALO**
Carob tree liqueur

**LICOR DE MANZANILLA**
Chamomile (and other herbs) liqueur

# SHOPPING

### FASHION & JEWELLERY

On Menorca and the other Balearic Islands, the stylish wear loose-fitting and comfortable but no less striking clothing made from cotton and linen in Mediterranean designs. Menorca's most famous label, *Pou Nou*, errs towards this classic look. If you're more interested in jewellery, *Lithica* (Stone Age) makes wonderful original pieces including necklaces and earrings in geometric designs that recall the island's history of quarrying *(lithica.es)*.

### KNOCK IT BACK

One of the most popular Menorcan souvenirs is its gin (a throwback to British rule). The dark brown, high-proof speciality *palo*, a liqueur made from melted sugar or carob tree fruit is also delicious (and strong!). *Hierbas* or *herbes*, a liqueur containing up to 40 different island herbs, actually comes from Ibiza, but you will find it in every bar on Menorca alongside Menorcan chamomile liqueur. Menorcan chamomile is more aromatic and bitter than its European cousin. The essential oils and resins stored in the flower are good for the stomach so it is no surprise a digestif made from it is the perfect way to round off a meal! Chamomile tea is also available …

**INSIDER TIP**
A herbal tea? You must be kidding

### CHEESY GIFTS

It has hardly any aroma, has a semi-firm rind and, because of its square shape, is easy to store and transport. *Queso Maó-Menorca* (as it has been officially called since 1995) is sold by companies such as *Coinga*, *Sant Patrici* and *La Payesa*. Menorcan cheese is an ideal gift which you can buy in most grocery stores or from a producer in Alaior. If you want to take back authentic Menorcan products, pay a visit to

A pair of classic leather *avarques* and some Menorcan chamomile are the perfect souvenirs

delis (*El Paladar*, for example) in Ciutadella and Maó who buy exclusively from local producers.

## PERUSE THE MARKETS ALL DAY (& EVENING) LONG

The old and new capitals and every decent-sized resort on Menorca are home to interesting markets *(mercat)* selling everything from food to crafts. As it can get too hot during the day, many take place in the evening, for example Maó's Tuesday market *(8-11pm)*. Further inland the markets often pay heed to the island's artisanal tradition. Such is the case in Alaior *(Wed 7-11pm)*, Es Migjorn Gran *(Tue 7-11pm)* and Es Mercadal *(Thu 7-10pm)*.

## A GOOD SOLE

Local cobblers can become global brands: Pons Quintana and Jaume Mascaró are every bit at home on Menorca as they are in New York, Milan or London. The local sandals that made their fame are back in in a big way: *avarques* with their flat rubber soles, ankle straps and 'toe holder' are now a part of an relaxed international look. You will find hundreds of different kinds, in every colour imaginable or covered in diamante so there's no excuse not to take a pair home!

INSIDER TIP
A good sole

# SPORT & ACTIVITIES

The mild Mediterranean climate makes getting outdoors for exercise possible all year round. Sea swimming is best between May and October, but all the major resorts offer far more than just beaches. From gyms and tennis courts to volleyball courts, minigolf courses, bike-hire shops and watersports centres, there is something for everyone. The "Menorca Activa" brochure *(menorcaactiva.com)* is a useful source of up-to-date information.

including the western and eastern parts of the island around Ciutadella and Maó. Bicycle, e-bike and mountain bike hire is available in both cities and in almost all the holiday resorts.

In Ciutadella *Velos Joan (from 12 euros per day | Carrer de Vila Juaneda Industrial | tel. 971 38 15 76 | velosjoan.com)* is your best bet; in Maó it is *Bike Menorca (from 15 euros per day | Avinguda de Francesc Femenías 44 | tel. 971 35 37 98 | bikemenorca.com)*. For the top cycling routes, see *menorca.es*.

## CYCLING

Although at first sight Menorca appears fairly flat, its many ascents will make riding tough for less experienced riders. The main roads are very busy, there are very few bicycle paths and lots of minor roads are in very poor condition. However, cycling can still be a real pleasure in certain areas,

## GOLF

In contrast to Mallorca (which has over 20 courses), Menorca is relatively poorly supplied. There is just one 18-hole course but it is very beautiful, set just off the coast in the north of the island. The green fee at *Golf Son Parc Menorca (open all year round | Urb. Son Parc s/n | Es Mercadal | tel.*

A yacht in Cales Coves

971 18 88 75 | *golfsonparc.com)* is 75.50 euros in July and August but it is considerably cheaper out of season or after 5pm.

## RIDING

More than a dozen riding schools (mostly inland) offer lessons and trail rides. At *Cavalls Son Àngel (Camí d'Algaiarens | Ciutadella | mobile tel. 609 83 39 02 | cavallssonangel.com)* you can book one-hour to five-day hacks, mainly on the Camí de Cavalls. And if you prefer to just watch, the two race-courses *Hipódrom Municipal (Ctra Maó–Sant Lluís | Sat 6pm in summer, Sun mornings in autumn)* and *Hipódrom Torre del Ram (Ciutadella | Urb. Torre del Ram | Sun 6pm)* organise trotting races every weekend.

## SAILING

Courses are available in Fornells, Son Xoriguer and Maó. You can hire larger yachts or sailing boats with or without a skipper at the ports in Maó, Ciutadella, Fornells, Cala en Bosc and S'Algar. The best option is *Windsurf Fornells (mobile tel. 664 33 58 01 | windfornells.com)*. On presentation of a valid sailing licence, you can hire sailing yachts and motorboats in Maó, for example at *Nautic Fun (Moll de Llevant 57 | tel. 971 36 42 50 | nauticfunmenorca.com)*.

## SPORTING EVENTS

Whether biking, hiking or swimming, Menorcans love to get involved in competitions; visitors are welcomed too. The *Trail dels Fars (traildelsfars.com)* is a 44-km run/walk beginning at the lighthouse *(far)* on the Cap de Cavalleria. The *Half Menorca (artiem halfmenorca.com)* takes place in September. It is a punchy triathlon with a 1.9-km swim, 90-km cycle and 21-km run. There is an easier version for the sensible/less brave. The sporting season ends in October with the *Vuelta a Menorca (menorcacicloturista. com)*, a lap of the island on bikes.

## TENNIS
All the major hotels have their own courts and tennis coaches are usually also available. Local public courts are also open to tourists.

## WALKING & HIKING
Most hotels will be able to suggest walks for their guests. There are hiking trails all over the island, but they are rarely signposted and often blocked by walls, locked gates and thorny vegetation. Hiking maps (obtainable in bookshops) are very useful, but not always accurate. Hiking clubs and other institutions organise hikes (usually in the off-season) in which non-members can also participate (ads in local press).

The 185-km coastal path ★ *Camí de Cavalls (camidecavalls360.com)* takes in dramatic cliffs, remote bays, pine forests and stunning beaches – and you always get a sea view.

INSIDER TIP
**A bit of everything**

This former "horse path" was created in the Middle Ages as a patrol path for the defence of the island from any point. It has been recently restored and is hugely popular with walkers; and there are plenty of ways to walk shorter stretches.

A good operator for guided walks is *Xauxa Menorca Reloaded (C/ Verge del Toro 10 | Es Mercadal | mobile tel. 685 74 73 08 | rutasmenorca.com)*. The hikes through the gorges of the Barranc d'Algendar are particularly impressive.

## WATER SPORTS
Menorca's stunning underwater world makes it a great place to go diving. More than its natural diversity, it's the water's incredible clarity and excellent visibility as well as the many underwater caves and shipwrecks that really make it special. There are more than 20 diving schools on the island and most offer courses in English. Almost all offer taster courses, PADI qualification and customised

excursions as well as equipment hire. One of the schools with the best locations is the German-run *Tauchschule Poseidon (in the Hostal Bahía | Cala Santandria | tel. 971 38 26 44 | bahia-poseidon.de)*, which sits directly on *Cala Santandria*'s beach. You can put on your wetsuit and dive straight in!

Windsurfing and kayaking are the next most popular water sports on the island. Water-skiing and paragliding are on offer in S'Algar and Cala en Bosc. Pedalos and small motorboats (for which you don't need a licence) are available on most beaches. You can rent kayaks and SUP boards on Cala Galdana and at Son Xoriguer, Es Grau and Fornell.

**INSIDER TIP**
**Sea like a millpond**

The calm waters and dramatic cliffs in the almost totally enclosed bay of Fornells are particularly well suited to aquatic exploration. *Dia Complert*'s guides *(Av. Passeig Maritim 41 | mobil tel. 609 67 09 96 | diacomplert.com)* lead tours through coastal caves and into unexplored bays, with time for you to snorkel or sunbathe. They have been around for over 20 years offering a huge range of water-based activities.

As you hike the Camí de Cavalls, the sound of the sea is always in your ears

# REGIONAL OVERVIEW

CIUTADELLA & THE WESTERN TIP p. 90

Cala Morell

Cala es Fontanell

Cala del Pilar

Cala Morell

Ciutadella

Cala Santandria

Ferreríes

Barranc de Santa Aina

**Beautiful beaches and a town to fall in love with**

Cala Blanca

Cala Galdana

Es Migjorn Gran

Cala en Bosc

Cala Macarella

Cala Galdana

Sant Tomas

**Forests, fields and picture-perfect beaches**

MIGJORN, CENTRE & THE SOUTH p. 76

Mar Mediterrània

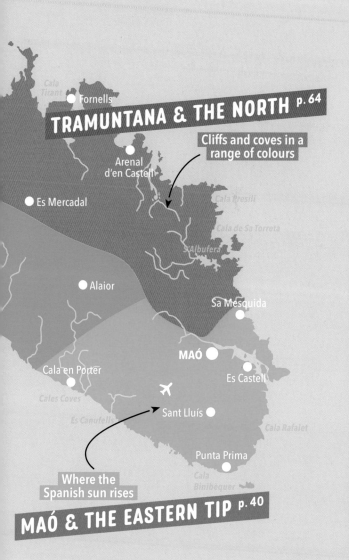

Cala Tirant

Fornells

**TRAMUNTANA & THE NORTH** p. 64

Cliffs and coves in a range of colours

Arenal d'en Castell

Cala Presili

Es Mercadal

Cala de Sa Torreta

S'Albufera

Alaior

Sa Mesquida

**MAÓ**

Es Castell

Cala en Porter

Cales Coves

Es Canufells

Sant Lluís

Cala Rafalet

Where the Spanish sun rises

Punta Prima

Cala Binibèquer

**MAÓ & THE EASTERN TIP** p. 40

5 km
3.11 mi

# MAÓ & THE EASTERN TIP

## A CAPITAL ON A BIG BAY

Maó owes its status as the island's capital to its large bay where ships have been able to anchor safely for hundreds of years. The city itself is large by Menorcan standards and is packed with Mediterranean charm. Its bustle presents a contrast to the peaceful holiday resorts that line the southern coast.

The rivalry between Maó and Ciutadella has a long history. The enmity between the east and the west of Menorca – between the old

The Church of Santa Maria in Maó stands firm in the Mediterranean breeze

and new capitals – has been smouldering for centuries. For many years, Ciutadella was the most important port on the island. That all changed with the arrival of the British who made Maó their capital in 1722. This so appalled the wealthy families of Ciutadella that they have been waging war with the "British city of Maó" ever since. In Maó itself, the Brits are treated almost as liberators who brought wealth through trade.

# MAÓ & THE EASTERN TIP

Me-1

**4** Talatí de Dalt

🚗 17km, 20 mins

Me-12

☀️ 🏖️ **14** Cala en Porter

● **Sant Climent** p. 6

E S P A Ñ A

**13** Cales Coves ★

**12** Es Canutells

Es Canutells

Binidali

*M a r*

*M e d i t e r r à n i a*

Binisafua

---

## MARCO POLO HIGHLIGHTS

★ **SANTA MARIA**
Admire the marvellous organ in this church in Maó – ideally at a concert ➤ p. 47

★ **TOUR OF PORT DE MAÓ**
Take a glass-bottomed boat around the Mediterranean's largest natural harbour ➤ p. 50

★ **BINIBÈQUER VELL**
A fascinating warren of narrow alleys full of nooks and crannies. A surprisingly well-designed resort ➤ p. 59

★ **CALES COVES**
The twin bay with its 100 caves has a turbulent past but today it's a place to kick back and relax ➤ p. 61

Me-7

Me-3

**5** Sa Mesquida

Tour of Port de Maó ★
Santa Maria ★

**Maó** p. 44

Cala Llonga

**1** Illa del Rei

Me-12

RM

**Es Castell**
p. 54

Me-4

**6** Illa del Llatzeret

**3** Talaiot de Trepucó

Sol d'Este

**2** La Mola

Llucmaçanes

**7**
Castell de
Sant Felip

Me-8

Me-6

15km, 19 mins

Trebaluger

6km, 10 mins

**Sant Lluís** p. 57

s'Ullestrar

15km, 20 mins

Me-10

Torret

Me-8

Cala Rafalot

**8** S'Algar

Binibèquer Vell ★

**9** Cala d'Alcalfar

**10** Punta Prima

Cala
Binibèquer

Son Ganxo

▲
N
2 km
1.24 mi

# MAÓ

*J6* **With only 29,500 inhabitants, Menorca's capital may seem small but, in fact, around half the island's population lives there. The city sits atop steep cliffs which form a fjord-like protected natural harbour and the pretty villas and colonial-era houses give Maó its particular charm.**

The city has much to offer in the way of culture, including Menorca's best museum, Spain's oldest opera house and several churches. It also has a long line of bars, restaurants and clubs to choose from along its regenerated quayside. It's worth spending a few days in Maó to see how Menorcans really live. The nearest beaches are just a few miles away and all of the island's resorts are easily accessible by bus or car.

Maó is divided into three distinct areas: the historic centre is in the upper part of the city, from where you can head down to the "seaside" district (Baixamar), with its line of restaurants and amusements along the quayside. On the "Other Side" (S'Altra Banda), that is to say on the north bank of the fjord, you'll find more sights. Most visitors first head to the Plaça de s'Esplanada with its bus station, car park and tourist information. The Carrer de ses Moreres on the eastern side of the square takes you to the Plaça d'Espanya with a set of steps leading down to the harbour. There is also a free lift near the *Port Mahon* hotel.

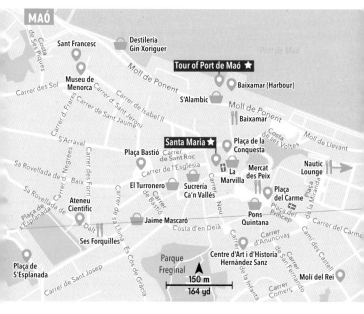

Maó's quayside lights up when the sun begins to set

## SIGHTSEEING

### BAIXAMAR (PORT)

"Julio, agosto y Maó/los mejores puertos del Mediterráneo son" (July, August and Maó are the best ports in the Mediterranean). At least this was the rhyme made up by Admiral Andrea Doria, and he should know. He spoke only in glowing terms of his favourite port. Adequate depth, excellent protection from storms for a whole fleet, and good medical provision are among the benefits of the 6-km-long and more than 1,000-m-wide harbour channel. Furthermore, the fortress of *Sant Felip* could block access making the harbour an ideal naval base, unique across the Mediterranean.

It is only fairly recently that the landlubbers of Maó have found more civilian uses for the port. Today you go "down to the sea" to *Baixamar* for a good time. The port promenade is home to a large number of restaurants and plenty of places organising activities and excursions. During the day it is the starting point for boat trips around the harbour and to the popular *Xoriguer* gin distillery (see p. 49). On weekend evenings the whole place is transformed, with nightclubs and bars pulling in punters from across the island.

However, Baixamar is not only the spruced-up area around the two harbour breakwaters – *Moll de Ponent*, to the west, extends east to *Moll de Llevant* – but also the stretch of coast to the north and opposite. This is where you'll find the capital's warehouses and industrial area as well as freight ship terminals. Unfortunately,

The former cloisters on Plaça del Carme now throng with shoppers and sightseers

Menorca's only power station also belches emissions here. The station provides part of the island with energy – the rest coming via undersea cable from Mallorca. *a–e1*

## SANT FRANCESC

The people of Maó also call this mighty church the "cathedral". It took almost a century to build (1719–92), during which time architectural fashion changed several times. Next to it is the *Museu de Menorca* housed in the former Franciscan convent *Sant Francesc*, founded in 1439. The road there is lined with stately buildings. *Plaça des Monestir* | 🕐 *15 mins* | *a1*

## MUSEU DE MENORCA 👕

A former monastery full of treasures: The Museum of Menorca contains many local artefacts, historic paintings and maps, as well as contemporary art. It serves as a repository of Menorca's traditions, customs and long history. The cloister of the 15th-century Franciscan monastery is also open to visitors. *June–Sept Tue–Sat 10am–2pm, 6–8pm, Sun 10am–2pm, Oct–May Tue, Thu 10am–6pm, Wed, Fri–Sun 10am–2pm | admission 4 euros | Tue, Thu and Sun free, temporary exhibitions also free | Plaça Pla des Monestir | museudemenorca.com | 🕐 at least 45 mins | a1*

## PLAÇA DE LA CONQUESTA

Here, in the oldest part of the town, is the *Casa de Cultura*, a cultural centre with public library and the town archive; a few steps further on is the *town hall* (construction began in

1789). From the end of the short alley-way *Carrer d'Alfons III* you can enjoy a lovely view over the port. *b1*

### SANTA MARIA ★

Built in 1748 on the ruins of an older church, at first glance Santa Maria seems a simple building which has more to offer the ear than the eye. Its grand organ is indeed a masterpiece of instrument making. In 1809 the German-Swiss organ builders Otter & Kyburz were given the commission and the instrument was delivered to Menorca in just one year. With its 3,120 pipes and four keyboards it was soon well known across the island, especially for its ability to imitate human singing. There are concerts almost every day, which will induce a sense of wonder in even the most sceptical visitors. It is well worth going to the first floor to see it up close. *Mon–Sat 9am–12.30pm, 3.30–7pm, 30 mins organ recital June–Oct Mon–Sat 1pm | admission to concert 5 euros, church 2 euros | between Plaça de la Conquesta and Plaça de la Constitució | 15 mins. | b1*

### PLAÇA BASTIÓ

From the bars and cafés, you'll spot a gate flanked by towers – formerly part of the city's medieval wall. This used to be the starting point for long journeys to Ciutadella, the western tip of the island, but today anyone who wants to head to the nearby bus station has to pass through it. *b1–2*

### PLAÇA DEL CARME

This is one spot everyone passes.

Maó's central square is named after the former *Claustre del Carme* convent whose colonnades (built from 1726) house souvenir shops and delis as well as some vegetable and fruit stands. Most produce is now sold in the modern basement where there is a supermarket popular with locals *(car park on the Plaça Miranda | mercat desclaustre.com)* The *Mercat des Peix*, the fish market between Plaça del Carme and Plaça d'Espanya, offers all the bounty of the sea. Try to arrive as early as you can to get the best selection. The little tapas bars and the beautiful views of the harbour below are a great reason to spend some time here *(Tue–Sat from 7.30am). b–c2*

### CENTRE D'ART I D'HISTORIA HERNÁNDEZ SANZ

Adorned with decorative murals, this restored merchants' house (1805) is a fine example of how Menorca's upper class once lived. The museum here is as interesting as the architecture, tracing the development of the harbour under British rule as well as exhibiting expressive paintings and etchings by Menorcan artists. The views from the tower are great! *Tue–Sun 10am–1.30pm, Thu and Sat also 6-8pm | admission 5 euros, free on Sun | C/ Anuncivay 2 | at least 30 mins | b1*

### MOLÍ DEL REI 🐖

"King's Mill", a mill tower dating from the 18th century, today houses a centre for ecological information, a shop with Menorcan souvenirs (usually environmentally friendly), and one of the best viewing platforms overlooking the old town and the port. *Mon–Fri 9.30am–2.30pm and Mon–Thu 5.30–8pm | admission free | Camí des Castell 53 | gobmenorca.com/moli | ⏱ 20 mins | ▥ c2*

*Reial*, home to the city's main theatre, *Teatro Principal*. Straight ahead is the city gate through which Ottoman corsair Hayreddin Barbarossa once forced his way into Maó before subjugating and plundering the town and

Civilised idleness in Maó's old town

### PLAÇA DE S'ESPLANADA

If you arrive by bus, this will be the starting point for your exploration of Maó. From Plaça de S'Esplanada, *Carrer de ses Moreres* – lined with bars and traditional shops – leads eastwards into the old part of the town. You'll also find a bronze bust of one of Maó's illustrious residents: Dr Mateu Orfila (1787–1853), famous among physicians as the father of toxicology, the study of poisons. At the end of the boulevard, *Carrer Bastió* forks off to the left, and if you go to the right you'll come to *Costa d'en Deia* and *Plaça*

abducting more than 1,000 inhabitants. Centuries later, a small number of the merchants are said to have opened the gate for the pirates in order to protect their own property. From the *plaça* heading north you come to the capital's bus station. ▥ a2

### ATENEU CIENTÍFIC

This cultural centre with its warm wooden and geometrically tiled floors is used by the Menorcans for relaxed social gatherings known as *tertulias*. Holidaymakers are more likely to visit small exhibitions of ceramics, antique maps and fossils. The concerts and cinema club are also interesting. *Sun-Fri 10am-2pm, 4-9pm, mornings only in summer | Sa Rovellada de Dalt 25 | near Plaça de S'Esplanada | ateneumao.org | ⏱ 30 mins | ⑭ a2*

## EATING & DRINKING

### BAIXAMAR

No matter when you get here, this quayside café with its black and white tiles, dark wooden furniture and gleaming mirrors will be full of people of every age and class. The food is not fancy but is delicious and you can wash it down with a *pomada* (gin and lemonade). *Daily from 9am | Moll de Ponent 17 | € | ⑭ b1*

### MERCAT DES PEIX

Central but well hidden: in the fish market you will find the very freshest local seafood, while tapas bars serve Menorcan specialities: mussels caught in the fjord, cold cuts and cheese from inland farms, and delicious pastries. *Mon-Sat 11.30am-3pm, 7.30-11pm | between Plaça del Carme and Plaça d'Espanya | €-€€| ⑭ b2*

INSIDER TIP
**Local delicacies**

### NAUTIC LOUNGE

INSIDER TIP
**BQ on a boat**

A truly unique culinary experience! Hop aboard this small, round boat with a barbecue in the middle and set off to explore the harbour while your food is cooking (no yachting licence required). You can choose from different menus ranging from BBQ to sushi. *Trips at lunch and in the evening | 300 Moll de Llevant | mobile tel. 609 30 04 59 | nauticlounge.com | €€€ | ⑭ 0*

### SES FORQUILLES

Oriol and Raquel's young team serve tasty, nicely presented dishes with a creative touch. Their speciality is Menorcan king prawns with truffles. They also do tapas in a lively bistro atmosphere. *Closed Tue and Wed evenings and Sun | Rovellada de Dalt 20 | tel. 971 35 27 11 | sesforquilles. com | €€ | ⑭ a2*

## SHOPPING

*Carrer Hannóver (⑭ b2)* or – as the Menorcans prefer – *Costa de Sa Plaça*, is Maó's main shopping street, but *Plaça Colón* with its palm trees and cobblestones also has lots to offer. This and *Carrer Nou* are the places to meet for a celebration or just a cup of coffee. A lovely *market* (including arts and crafts) is held on *Tue and Sat 9am-2pm on Plaça de S'Esplanada (⑭ a2)*. The night market *Mercat de Nit (⑭ b-c2) (July/Aug Tue 8-11pm | Plaça del Carmen | ⑭ b-c2)* is even more attractive.

### DESTILERÍA GIN XORIGUER

You will see Gin Xoriguer everywhere on Menorca. But it is produced here in Maó's port. You can sample it at source and also buy a bottle in a decorative design. Try the herbal liqueurs, too! To this very day, the Pons family keeps the recipe under lock and key. Around

60 per cent of production is consumed on the island, either neat or as *pomada* (gin and lemonade). *Andén de Poniente 91 (branch in the old town: Plaça del Carme 16) | xoriguer.es | ▥ a1*

### EL TURRONERO

If you are looking for edible souvenirs, this is a gold mine. The range of products not only includes sweets *(turrones)* and excellent ice cream, but also cheese and cold meats. *C/ Nou 22–24 | ▥ b2*

### JAIME MASCARÓ

Your suitcase definitely has space for one more pair of shoes! With bold designs (for belts and bags too) this is Menorca's most famous brand. *C/ Ses Moreres 29 | jaimemascaro.es*

### LA MARVILLA

Nice, small gift shop in the centre. What separates it from the crowd is the friendly-looking Menorcan mule whinnying on their cups, aprons and T-shirts. *C/ Portal del Mar 7 | ▥ b1–2*

### PONS QUINTANA

Wacky women's shoes from pink pumps to turquoise cowboy boots. *C/ S'Arravaleta 21 | ponsquintana.com | ▥ b2*

### S'ALAMBIC

You can buy typical Menorcan souvenirs here in a typical Menorcan building: ceramics, jewellery, clothing and leather goods. *Moll de Ponent 36 | ▥ b1*

### SUCRERÍA CA'N VALLÉS

This is where cake connoisseurs reckon you can get the best *ensaïmadas* in town, as well as other traditional tasty pastries. *C/ Hannóver 16 | ▥ b2*

## SPORT & ACTIVITIES

### BOAT TRIPS

Strolling down Maó's promenades is wonderful, but seeing the city from the water is even better so don't miss out on a ★ *port cruise* (◷ 1 hr). Try and get down to the steps on the quay early to avoid the crowds. *Líneas de la Cruz (several cruises daily Mon–Sat during summer | ticket 12 euros | tickets tel. 971 35 07 78 | rutas maritimasdelacruz.com)* runs trips on *Don Joan*, sailing you around the natural harbour for an hour, while you look through the underwater windows and listen to the commentary.

*Líneas de la Cruz* also organises half-day excursions to remote bays and beaches, some of which are otherwise inaccessible. Tours start from Maó and head northeast via Sa Mesquida to Illa d'en Colom and the Es Grau Nature Reserve as well as south via Punta Prima and Binibèquer to Canutells, with breaks for a swim in summer *(in summer daily 10am and 2.30pm, return approx. 1pm and 5.30pm).*

### SAILING

You can book sailing trips and hire boats using the following companies: *Menorca Náutica (Moll de Llevant 163 | tel. 971 35 45 43 | menorcanautic. com); Blue Mediterraneum (Moll de*

Llevant | mobile tel. 609 30 52 14); Menorca Cruising School (Moll de Levant 303 | Sant Lluís | mobile tel. 6 60 64 78 45 | menorcasailing.co.uk) also offers lessons.

### NIGHTLIFE

*Nits de Música al Carrer* is great fun. Every Tuesday evening in summer *(late June–late Aug, 9–11.30 pm | FB:*

A boat trip gives you a different view of Maó's harbour

### TENNIS

Need a bit of exercise after a long day at the beach? There are floodlit courts at *Tenis Mahón (C/ Trepucó 4 | tel. 971 36 05 76).*

### BEACHES

There are no beaches in Maó itself but there are lots of pretty places not far away such as Sa Mesquida, Punta Prima and Cala en Porter.

*nitsdemusicaalcarrer)* many shops stay open after hours, restaurants offer cheap tapas, and live bands deliver the perfect backdrop of sound, with funk, fusion and flamenco. Young people will find lots of action in the western port area around *Moll de Ponent*, with bars, cafés and pubs staying open all night long. The most popular one with locals is the cosy *Baixamar* (see p. 49),

**INSIDER TIP**
**An evening of live music**

while *Sa Terrassa des Claustre (Fri–Sat, sometimes Sun | Pati del Claustre del Carme s/n | esclaustre.com)* is an unusual – almost sacred – venue housed in an old monastery. The central courtyard is transformed into a buzzing concert hall with a mixture of live acts and DJs every weekend, with local food available in the *Refectori*.

The eastern port district round *Moll de Llevant* has a more sedate and international feel. One institution is *Bar Nou (C/ Nou 1)*. Housed in an art nouveau building in the upper part of the city close to Santa María, this bar serves cocktails in a quiet, old-school setting with a pretty outside seating area. In the old town *Cristianal i Gradinata (Tue–Sat 7-11.30pm | C/ Isabel II)* is a jazz and blues bar run by Señor Chiqi. From its terrace (just a few steps away from the Mirador des ses Monges) the city's harbour spreads out below you. Last but not least, music lovers should not miss out on a concert at the ☂ *Teatre (Costa Deia 40 | teatremao.com)* Spain's oldest opera house with its wonderful architecture and acoustics.

A must for fans of classical music: a concert in Maó's opera house

# AROUND MAÓ

## 1 ILLA DEL REI
*1.5km east of Maó / 20 mins (by boat)*

Governor Kane commissioned the construction of a huge hospital complex which to this day covers a large part of the small island in the Port de Maó bay. From its construction in the 18th century until the 1950s, the building was used as a hospital. The island, which British seafarers christened *Bloody Island* 200 years ago, is shrouded in dark tales – including stories of the surgical "waste" that used to be thrown into the sea here.

In 1986, Maó council announced they were going to take on the building and there was talk transforming it into a genetic research centre or a museum; Elton John was also interested in buying it, while other plans included a hotel and R&D centre for the electricity company. However, to this day the building stands empty.

There are also the remains of an early Christian basilica on Illa del Rei though its main attraction, a relatively well-preserved mosaic, is exhibited in the *Museu de Menorca* in Maó. The small island owes its regal name to Alfonso III of Aragón who landed there in 1287 and held out until reinforcements arrived to retake Menorca from the hands of the Moorish occupying forces. *2½-hr tour from Maó Moll de Levant April–Sept only, Sun 8.45am and 10.45am with the "Yellow Submarine" | ticket 10 euros | isla hospitalmenorca.org |* 🗺 *J–K6*

## 2 LA MOLA 🚩
*11km southeast of Maó / 18 mins (by car on the Me-3)*

Both the French and British occupiers of the island considered transforming the strategically important peninsula at the entrance to the bay of Maó into a bastion. However, the present fortress complex was constructed from 1850–60 after the demolition of the castle of San Felipe by the Spaniards. After Queen Isabella II of Bourbon visited the fort, it was christened "Fortaleza Isabel II". However, the fortress has never seen any military action, which is why it is so perfectly preserved. Today there is a full range of activities on offer from guided tours *(6 euros)* and bike rides to buggy safaris *(30 mins | 25 euros)*, concerts, plays and dance performances. You will find the current events calendar at: *fortalesalamola.com. Access via Port de Maó, Ctra La Mola, 7km | May–Sept 10am–8pm, Oct and April 10am–6pm, Nov–March 10am–2pm | admission 8 euros |* ⏱ *at least 1 hr |* 🗺 *K6*

## 3 TALAIOT DE TREPUCÓ 🐗
*3.5km south of Maó / 9 mins (by car on the Camí de Trepucó)*

This prehistoric settlement is often described as the site with the most spectacular megalith in the Balearics, the *taula* (more than 4.2m), and with the largest *talaiot* construction (40m). It's believed that the settlement was founded around 1700 BCE and extended far beyond the "holy shrine". Today, you can still see remnants of the settlement beyond the enclosing wall. *Admission free | ⏲ 30 mins | ▥ J6*

#### 4 TALATÍ DE DALT
*4.5km west of Maó / 8 mins (by car on the Me-1)*

You'll find the ruins of this ancient settlement in a windswept landscape of olive and fig trees. Climb over the enclosing wall and transport yourself back to an era when animals were sacrificed on the enormous *taula*. The animals were probably kept in the caves, which they entered via l arge openings. The access road is signposted (main road Maó– Ciutadella, 4km). *10am–sunset | admission 4 euros | Nov-March free | disfrutamenorca.com/talati-de-dalt | ⏲ 30 mins | ▥ H6*

#### 5 SA MESQUIDA 🏖
*7km northeast of Maó / 12 mins (by car on the Me-3)*

This is where the people of Maó come to swim and sunbathe on a stunning white beach set against black slate cliffs. The 700m of coastline here is divided into two by a headland. The larger beach is around 300m long and has a hefty tower on it. In 1781 Sa Mesquida was the starting point of the Franco-Spanish reconquest, which gave the British reason enough to secure the bay with its own fortification (1798). Restaurant tip: *Cap Roig (April–Oct daily | C/ de Sa Mesquida 13 | tel. 971 18 83 83 | €–€€)*, which has an inviting terrace overlooking the sea.

# ES CASTELL

▥ *J-K6* **There may be lots of Castells but there is only one Es Castell (pop. 7,900). It was first called Georgetown by the British before a period as Villacarlos and then it finally settled on its current name.**

As you make your way along the mile-long "fjord" which ends in Maó, you will see the traces of British colonial rule in the architecture of Es Castell: a rectangular town plan and a central main square surrounded by garrison buildings.

The highlight of this small town is the tranquil harbour, *Cales Fonts*. Colourful boats bob at anchor, surrounded by charming bars and restaurants that are always packed with people who have come from Maó. And the mornings are special here too – this is where you get the first rays of sun in Spain. There is no town further east in the whole country.

## EATING & DRINKING

### ANA LUISA
At *Ana Luisa*, aka *Francisco*, you'll know you're at the seaside: enjoy their paella loaded with prawns and calamari. Veggies will also find a wide selection of delicious dishes. *Closed Wed | C/ Moll d'en Pons (just below Hotel Hamilton) | tel. 649 08 36 75 | €€*

### CAPRICHOSA
Harbour view: trendy pizzeria which also serves an affordable set menu. *C/ Cales Fonts 44 | tel. 971 36 61 58 | €€*

Just a crumbling wall? Nope! Prehistoric settlement ruins in Talatí de Dalt

### DINKUMS BAR-RESTAURANTE

It's a hell of a location – built into the cliffs with a view over the harbour. And in the evenings, it is lit by candles. Get Peter and José to tell you what the best fish of the day is. *C/ Cales Fonts 20 | tel. 971 36 70 17 | €€–€€€*

**INSIDER TIP** *For fresh fish fans*

### EL CHIVITO

The ideal place for a light snack: very good value, friendly and tasty. They serve delicious *bocadillos*. Popular with a young clientele. *Daily | C/ Cales Fonts 25 | tel. 971 35 29 44 | €*

### IRENE

Hearty Menorcan cuisine with the freshest ingredients in a pretty restaurant. The terrace has a stunning view of the bay and they do a good and very reasonable lunch menu. *C/ de Sa Font 1 | tel. 971 35 47 88 | €€*

## SHOPPING

There is a small artisan market on the port steps at *Cales Fonts* from June to September *(daily 8pm–2am)*. The *Mercat Artesanal (Mon 7pm–midnight | C/ Miranda des Cales Fonts)* offers exclusive arts and crafts.

## SPORT & ACTIVITIES

You can book a water taxi to take a private tour around the harbour or to ferry you across to Maó, the La Mola fortress or the Illa del Rei: *Water Taxi (15 April–15 Oct | tel. 616 42 88 91 | minimum of 2 persons, tickets are sold*

are the perfect setting for an evening cocktail. While sipping, you can watch boats chugging in and out of the harbour. The relaxed *Chèspir (C/ Cales Fonts 47)* regularly offers live jazz – and if you don't like cocktails, you can always order a smoothie. At *Lemon (C/ Cales Fonts 12)*, the atmosphere is

Bars, shops and restaurants line the port at Es Castell

*on board | watertaximenorca.com).* If you want to take the helm yourself, you can learn how to sail at the *Club Náutico Es Castell (Miranda de Cales Fonts | tel. 971 36 58 84).*

## NIGHTLIFE

Along the pedestrian promenades in Moll des Pons and Cales Fonts, small bars built into the rocks with terraces

definitely chilled.

The cave bar *Es Cau (daily from 10pm | C/ Cala Corb 5)* has been popular with Menorcans for decades partly thanks to its folk music. It sits in the not especially pretty bay of Cala Corb, 400m to the north-west. When David grabs his guitar, everyone gets up off their seats …

INSIDER TIP
**A singing landlord!**

# AROUND ES CASTELL

## 6 ILLA DEL LLATZERET

*800m east of Es Castell/only accessible by boat as part of a 2½-hr tour.*
The name says it all: "Hospital Island" – strategically located at the harbour entrance – was home to the largest hospital in the Mediterranean. From 1817–1917 this was the port quarantine centre. Heavily guarded and protected by massive walls, the hospital cared for patients with infectious diseases, such as the victims of the 1821 yellow fever and tetanus epidemic. In addition to the hospital, which is today used as a civil service spa and as a congress venue, there is a small *museum*. You can reach the island by boat from Es Castell as part of a tour lasting two hours 30 minutes (in English) *(15 July–31 Aug Tue 5–7.30pm, Thu, Sat 10am–12.30pm, Sun 5–7.30pm | tour 18 euros | lazaretodemahon.es)*; *cultural events* such as open-air film screenings and concerts are often held here *(nanventura.es)*. 🕮 *K6*

## 7 CASTELL DE SANT FELIP 🚩

*2km southeast of Es Castell / 4 mins (by car on the Me-6)*
The road to the cemetery *(Camí del Cementeri)* also leads (beyond the turn-off to Cala Sant Esteve) to the ruins of the fortress which once guarded the entrance to Port de Maó. Spain's King Philip II saw only one means of defence against the constant threat from pirates: the construction of a castle. Building started in 1554. The British later extended it into one of the most secure fortifications in the Mediterranean. After the reconquest in 1782, Charles III had it destroyed. What could possibly have driven him to that?

Today you can see ruins which are slowly but surely being reconquered, by nature this time. There are also underground tunnels and corridors to explore *(June–Sept Thu and Sun 10am 2-hr guided tours, otherwise only with pre-booking | admission 5 euros, night visit by torchlight 6 euros | tel. 971 36 21 00 | museomilitarmenorca.com/san-felipe)*.

Another impressive fortress protects the southern shore of the nearby Cala Sant Esteve. The British built the 18th-century 🚩 *Fort Marlborough (June–Oct Mon/Tue 10am–3pm, Wed–Sun 9.30am–7.30pm, April/May Tue–Sat 9.30am–3pm | admission 6 euros with audio guide | Mon free entrance | Cala Sant Esteve | the path from the car park has no shade and is long; try and drive all the way to the entrance)*; today its museum – with dark corridors, flickering candlelight, canon fire and more – will transport you back to the world of the war-torn 18th century. 🕮 *K6*

# SANT LLUÍS

🕮 *J7* **To honour Sant Lluís, this immaculately clean town has buildings painted white and neat**

Let yourself drift through the canyon-like cove of Cala Rafalet near S'Algar

as a pin, and the roads are well-maintained. It is almost too tranquil.

The town was founded by Count Lannion, erstwhile French governor, on a flying visit in the 18th century. Designed with a pencil and ruler, the town's layout is geometrical. The church, which gave the place its name, was dedicated to the French King Louis IX. Today, foreigners and people fleeing their hectic lives in Maó are most likely to settle here, which is why the city has a number of excellent restaurants. In the restored 🐷 mill (Tue–Sat 10am–1pm and 5–8pm | free admission| ajsantlluis.org) at the northern entrance to the town, you can learn more about the traditional milling industry.

## EATING & DRINKING

### LA RUEDA

Cheap tapas and set menus – no wonder it is often packed here at lunch. Simple furnishings, noisy, good vibes! Closed Tue | C/ Sant Lluís 30 | tel. 9 71 15 03 49 | €€

### PAN Y VINO

The 200-year-old country estate in the hamlet of Torret (on the way to the coast) is pure relaxation. Enjoy creative Mediterranean-Menorcan cuisine and – thanks to Patrick and Noelia – top-notch service in an elegant, modern country home with a pretty veranda. Sometimes there's live jazz in the

**INSIDER TIP**
Fusion food the Menorca way

evenings. *Closed Tue and at lunch | Camí de la Coixa 3 (Torret) | towards Punta Prima, Km6 | tel. 971 15 0322 | panyvinomenorca.com | €€€*

### SA PEDRERA D'ES PUJOL

Daniel and Nuria serve up original dishes n this cosy Torret restaurant that features light sandstone walls reminiscent of an old quarry. Their creative cuisine is rounded off by an extensive wine list. *Daily | Camí des Pujol 14 | towards Punta Prima, Km6 | tel. 971 15 07 17 | sapedreradespujol.com | €€€*

# AROUND SANT LLUÍS

### 8 S'ALGAR

*5km southeast of Sant Lluís / 7 mins (by car on the Me-8)*

No proper beach? That can be a good thing! In this coastal village, you climb down ladders from the rocks into the water, and it seems to keep mass tourism at bay even in the high season. Rather than roasting on the beach, try participating in some water sports – the possibilities are infinite. *Club S'Algar Diving (Passeig Marítin | tel. 971 15 06 01 | salgardiving.com)* offers almost every type of aquatic activity, and the hiring out diving equipment and sailing boats. If you fancy peace and quiet in a natural setting, you can walk round to the little cove *Cala Rafalet* via the high coastal path. *K7*

### 9 CALA D'ALCALFAR

*4km southeast of Sant Lluís / 7 mins (by car on the Me-8)*

This is how the fishing villages on the island once looked. Cala d'Alcalfar (or Alcaufar) is a simple village, mainly inhabited by Menorcans, with white boat houses by the sea. A natural breakwater at the entrance to the *cala* ensures calm sea. *K7*

### 10 PUNTA PRIMA

*5km south of Sant Lluís / 8 mins (by car on the Me-8)*

Even from a distance, you will be struck by the almost mirage-like turquoise sea; the striking colour – the result of the white limestone – is perfectly complemented by the red and white lighthouse on the small *Illa de l'Aire*, the "island of the air". Take some extra time to enjoy the beautiful vista from the viewpoint (signposted) on the west side of the bay (Punta de Mabres). Punta Prima has a big white sandy beach that gently drops down to the sea. It might not seem as romantic as other bays, but it's family-friendly, so is popular and can get busy. *J7*

### 11 BINIBÈQUER VELL ★

*4.5km southwest of Sant Lluís / 8 mins (by car on the Me-10)*

The main tourist attraction on the southeast coast is a like a rabbit warren. This "typical fishing village" actually came off the architectural drawing board in 1972, but the labyrinthine passages, tunnels, junctions and alcoves are so cleverly designed that they feel as if they've developed organically over centuries. Prior to the start of the season, the complex sparkles in pristine white – the natural stone floors are polished and souvenir shops tart up their windows. In peak season it gets crowded in the narrow streets. You can enjoy tapas, fresh fish and excellent chocolate cake in the *Club Náutico (daily | Passeig del Mar 29 | near Hotel Eden, right by the sea | nauticobinisafua.com | €€)*, where the atmosphere is relaxed and the sunsets superb. The beach bar *Bucaneros (Platja de Binibèquer | €)* is also an excellent place to treat yourself to a cool beer under a bamboo umbrella. There's always live music at the full moon in the *Bar Paupa (Cala Torret | C/ de Platja de Llevant | €€)*. 📖 *J7*

# SANT CLIMENT

📖 *H6* **If it weren't for the nearby airport, you might think you were in the countryside.**

But there aren't many planes taking off and landing in Menorca, so the Menorcan middle class have built lovely houses for themselves in this idyllic area. Check out the *Basílica des Fornas de Torelló* with its sixth-century mosaic and the *Talaiot de Torelló* (both to the left of the Sant Climent–Maó main road, just before the turn-off to the airport). The remarkable *Curnia* estate with its art nouveau design is not far away; it is said to have been created by a pupil of Gaudí. There is another *talaiot (Talaiot de Curnia | 2.8km)* behind the main building.

## EATING & DRINKING

### ES MOLÍ DE FOC
Dinner at a mill? Good food with French influences in the charming setting of a restored mill with an in-house brewery. *Daily | C/ Sant Llorenç 65 | tel. 971 15 32 22 | esmolidefoc.es | €€*

### RESTAURANTE CASINO SANT CLIMENT
Here you can enjoy an evening meal in a relaxed but classical dining room. There is live jazz on Tuesdays in summer from 8.30pm. *Daily | C/ Sant Jaume 4 | tel. 971 15 34 18 | casinosantcliment.com | €€–€€€*

**INSIDER TIP**
*Jazzy food*

## SHOPPING

You will find food and pastries on the Sant Jaume thoroughfare, and good cheese *(Quesos de Sant Climent)* in the C/ Sant Llorenç.

# AROUND SANT CLIMENT

## 🗺 ES CANUTELLS
*6km southwest of Sant Climent / 9 mins (by car on Ctra Binidalí)*
For the inhabitants of Sant Climent this bay is their village "port". It's

Stunning backdrop in radiant white: Binibèquer Vell

lovely on the seafront, where the boat-houses carved into the cliffs and a set of weathered stairs leading to the small beach stand as reminders of a bygone Menorca. In recent years a resort has developed above the bay extending deep inland. Only the western edge remains as it once was. On the road from Sant Climent to Sant Lluís, you can still admire a lovely example of Menorcan hybrid architecture: the 19th-century *Casat de Formet (Forma Vell)* mansion is impressive with its red façade, beautifully terraced garden and its fountains. *G–H7*

### 🔟 CALES COVES ⭐
*6.5km west of Sant Climent / 20 mins (by car on the Camí de Farana & Camí de Cales Coves)*

The Cales Coves ("Cave Bays") are a particularly great place to swim, sunbathe and relax. The cliffs keep the wind at bay and the water is crystal clear. Time seems to have a different rhythm here – a few dips and the day has gone … Three thousand years ago early settlers buried their dead here and a clan of latter-day hippies lived here until the mid-1990s. The place name is in the plural because the bay is divided into two; one half has a freshwater spring but both are deeply buried into the brown rock. The gravel path to get there is a bit bumpy. A more enjoyable route is to follow the red-signposted GR-223 trail from Cala en Porter on foot *(start at the mirador; the hike takes almost 2 hrs one way).*

There are around 100 caves and they have a complex past. The oldest date from the 11th century BCE and were used as burial sites. Up to the fourth century BCE larger caves were dug into the limestone rock, often with a central supporting column, benches and niches. They were also used as burial sites. Roman artefacts have been found here too. Some of the caves were used for ritual purposes and seafarers – including buccaneers – and fishermen repeatedly used the bay as a shelter in rough seas. *G6*

Disco with thrill factor: Cova d'en Xoroi

## 🔟 CALA EN PORTER 🌴

*7km west of Sant Climent / 10 mins (by car on the Me-12)*

On the left (as you look from the sea) the coast is natural and unspoilt, while on the right a holiday resort extends up the slope. The beach at the end of the bay is very broad, with fine sand sloping down gently to the sea – ideal for the whole family. However, beware, the word is out! The *Cova d'en Xoroi (May/Oct daily 3pm–sundown, June–Sept daily 11.30am–sundown; night sessions May–Oct daily from 11pm (18+ only) | admission incl. drink 11am–5pm, 10 euros, 20 euros after this | C/ de Sa Cova 2 | tel. 971 37 72 36 | covadenxoroi.com)* pulls in the punters with its unique location in a natural grotto and atmosphere. Halfway between sea and sky, on the steep slopes of the coastal cliffs, it provides a breathtaking view of the sea. It's particularly beautiful at sunset. The cliffs glow in the golden light, and fishing boats chug by while the seagulls sailing across the sky are practically close enough to touch. And when night falls, themed parties begin – from dolce vita to hippie chic.

It's no wonder this place has acquired its own legend. The Moorish pirate Xoroi ("the one-eared"), who was left behind by his crew on the coast of Menorca after a raid, is said to have used it as a base. Word spread among the peasants that there was a bandit in hiding: some hens went missing, then a pig. And one day a beautiful young girl disappeared. The peasants only discovered the thief's hiding place years later when, one winter's night, some snow had fallen on the fields and footprints led them to the cave. They stormed the pirate's cave and he hurled himself into the sea. They found the young woman in the best of health and with three children...

The area's top restaurant is the *Brasserie & Bar Dos Pablos (May–Oct daily from 6.30am | C/ de la Mediterrània 3 | tel. 971 37 79 12 | FB: brasseriebardospablos | €€–€€€)*. The British owners have managed to dispel all prejudice about English food and their excellent cuisine delights Menorcans as well as tourists. They are constantly adding new and wonderful creations to their repertoire. ⌖ *g6*

> **INSIDER TIP**
> **Dine with a pair of Pauls**

---

## WHERE TO STAY IN MAÓ & THE EAST

### DESIGN DREAM

This art nouveau palace, *Jardi de ses Bruixes (7 rooms | C/ de Sant Ferrán 26 | Maó | tel. 971 36 31 66 | hotelsesbruixes.com | €€ | ⌖ c2)*, has been redesigned by its trendy young architect owner. Each room has its own charm with lots of original elements and most are en suite.

### A COUNTRY IDYLL

Have breakfast in a charming garden! *Biniarroca (18 rooms | Camí Vell 57 | 2km north of Sant Lluís | tel. 971 15 00 59 | biniarroca.com | €€–€€€ | ⌖ J6)* is a romantic rural hideaway with two bougainvillea-bedecked pools.

# TRAMUNTANA & THE NORTH

## THE ISLAND'S WILD COAST

"The Tramuntana does not rest and does not forgive," says a Menorcan proverb, and when you see the cliffs – whose stone has been weathered by storm and spray over 400 million years – and the deformed pine trees bent by the northerly winds, you will immediately agree.

Over the years, hundreds of galleons and fishing boats have been wrecked off the rugged coast between Punta Nati and Cap de

The lighthouse at Cap de Cavalleria overlooks the wind-tossed seas of the north coast

Favàritx. The Tramuntana does not only shape rock and wood, but also its inhabitants; the people from the north coast tend to be quieter and more introspective than those from the south. The tough northerly winds can get you down, but they usually only blow fiercely from October to April. And the north is home to some of the nicest beaches on the whole island: Cala Tirant, Port d'Addaia, Arenal de Son Saura, Cala Pregonda, Na Macaret.

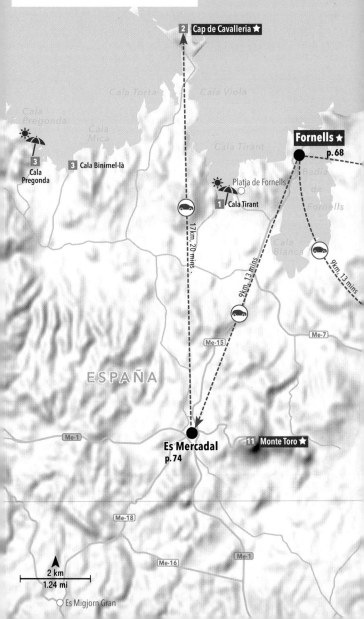

# TRAMUNTANA & THE NORTH

**2** Cap de Cavalleria ★

Cala Torta

Cala Viola

Cala Pregonda

Cala Mica

Cala Tirant

**Fornells ★**
p. 68

**3** Cala Pregonda

**3** Cala Binimel·là

Platja de Fornells

**1** Cala Tirant

Badia de Fornells

17km, 20 mins

9km, 13 mins

Cala Blanca

9km, 13 mins

Me-7

Me-15

ESPAÑA

Me-1

**11** Monte Toro ★

**Es Mercadal**
p. 74

Me-18

Me-1

Me-16

2 km
1.24 mi

Es Migjorn Gran

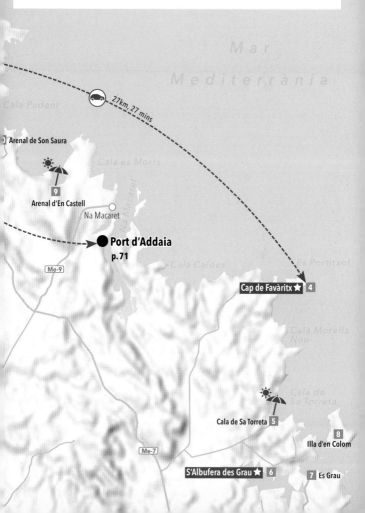

Mar Mediterrània

Cala Pudent

27km, 27 mins

Arenal de Son Saura

Cala es Morts

9
Arenal d'En Castell

Na Macaret

● **Port d'Addaia**
p. 71

Me-9

Cala Caldes

Es Portitxol

Cap de Favàritx ★ 4

Cala Morella Nou

Cala de Sa Torreta

Cala de Sa Torreta 5

8
Illa d'en Colom

Me-7

S'Albufera des Grau ★ 6

7 Es Grau

# FORNELLS

*▯ G2* **Even the Spanish royal family occasionally enjoys a ▸ *caldereta* (lobster in vegetable stock) here. ★ Fornells is famous for it. And the setting is perfect too: a lovely, quiet lagoon on the otherwise rugged northern coast with the old fishing port whose lobster fishermen are said to be the best in the western Mediterranean.**

In this context "best" doesn't only refer to the size of the catch – superb seafood is grilled and poached daily in all the local restaurants – but also to their careful management of the *langosta*: they have limited themselves to a season from April to August. Fornells itself dates back to the 17th century. When King Philip IV had a small fortress erected at the entrance to the bay in 1625, fishermen and their families (as well as a priest) soon settled in a row of houses.

## SIGHTSEEING

### SA TORRE DE FORNELLS

The island's most important defensive tower was once of 164 such structures on Menorca, erected by the British as a defence against their French opponents in the western Mediterranean. Today, it offers a spectacular view of the coast and lagoon. A small interactive exhibition tells its story. *May–Oct Tue–Sun 11am–2pm, 5–8pm | admission 2.50 euros | ⏱ 15 mins*

## EATING & DRINKING

### ES CRANC

"The Crab" is not located directly on the seafront but is still a popular destination. Ask about prices before ordering, though, as you will only be handed a menu if you ask for one. Tasty fish dishes, good *caldereta* and efficient service. *Daily | C/ Escoles 31 | tel. 971 37 64 42 | €€€*

### SA XERXA

There is a great view over the bay from the terrace and the food fits perfectly into the ambience with mussels, calamari, local prawns – and, of course *caldereta*. *Daily 12–5pm, Fri–Tue also 6.30–10pm | Passeig Maritim Gumersind Riera 9 | tel. 971 53 89 34 | €€–€€€*

## SPORT & ACTIVITIES

### BOAT TRIPS

Excursions to *Marina Norte*, the marine nature reserve to the west of Fornells, are strictly regulated. *Dia Complert (Av. Passeig Marítim 41 | tel. 609 67 09 96 | diacomplert.com)* are the experts, running tours with high-performance dinghies for up to 11 people, including a break for snorkelling. The contrast of the azure water against the red or orange cliffs is spectacular. The three-hour boat trip costs 60 euros per person (incl. soft drinks). You'll pay less than half of that at *Menorca Nord (in the summer daily 10am and 2pm | 28 euros | C/ Gurmesind Riera 98 |*

**INSIDER TIP**
**A colourful day out**

Take in the expansive sea view from the Torre de Fornells

mobile tel. 653 87 61 34 | menorca nord.com). For a small fee, they'll also pick you up from your hotel (40 euros).

## WATER SPORTS

Diving Center Fornells (Passeig Marítim 68 | tel. 971 37 64 31 | mobile tel. 619 41 41 51 | divingfornells.com) organises interesting dives on the north coast and also offers diving lessons. Expert staff will teach you how to sail, stand-up paddleboard and windsurf at Wind Fornells (at the harbour | mobile tel. 664 335801 | windfornells.com) and you can also hire sailing dinghies, catamarans and surfboards for solo adventures. The calm waters in the lagoon are ideal for trips with

> **SIDER TIP**
> **Like a millpond**

a kayak or stand-up paddleboard, even if you have little to no experience. You can hire both at Katayak (Passeig Marítim 69 | mobile tel. 626 48 64 26 | katayak.net) on the promenade. Dia Complert (see "Boat Trips") offers smaller boats too.

## NIGHTLIFE

### ISABELLA

Fornells' beach club is the ideal place for a stylish sunset cocktail: chairs in the sand, a drink in your hand, and a view of the setting sun. And sometimes there is relaxed live music – typical for Menorca. "Rather than techno, we prefer getting a violinist to play

> **INSIDER TIP**
> **The sound of the island**

Salines salt pans. A cluster of little white holiday homes climbs up the eastern slope of the bay, whilst the western side is undeveloped. From the broad, sandy beach, you'll have a view of sloping, unspoiled cliffs. On a clear night, the stars here are spectacular – that's why astronomers love Menorca! *F2–3*

**INSIDER TIP**
**Stargazing from the beach**

### 2 CAP DE CAVALLERIA ★

*15km northwest of Fornells / 23 mins (by car on the Camí de Tramuntana and Ctra Camides Far)*

The drive to Menorca's northern cape over windswept steppes is an adventure in itself – you might even meet a few wild goats. The view from around the lighthouse, which stands proudly on this northern cape, is simply stunning. To the left, over massive drops, you can see the rocky *Illa des Porros*; to the right is Cap de Fornells; towards the north, the view extends far over the sea to the horizon; towards the south you'll see the fjord-like *Cala Tirant* and inland to *Monte Toro*, Menorca's highest mountain.

If you're interested, you can also visit an exhibition on Menorca's five lighthouses in the former caretaker's cottage *(in the summer daily 10.30am–8.30pm | admission 3 euros)*. The beaches west of the cape are sensational. The wild, romantic *Platja de Cavalleria* (or *Ferragut*), the *Cala Binimel·là* and the *Cala Pregonda* are connected to the *Camí de Cavalls* path (see also p. 118). *F2*

Wild goats roam the northern cape

something classical or a saxophonist to do some jazz", says the owner, Xavier. *C/ Tramuntana | mobil tel. 638 78 54 80 | isabellamenorca.com*

# AROUND FORNELLS

### 1 CALA TIRANT

*8km southwest of Fornells / 13 mins (by car on the Me-15)*

Another stunning bay, this time cut so deep into the northern coast that it's safe to swim here. Take the road to the left just outside Fornells, near the Ses

### 🖪 CALA BINIMEL·LÀ & CALA PREGONDA

*12km west of Fornells / 23 mins (by car on the Camí de Tramuntana)*

Cala Binimel·là is only accessible via a dirt road. Enjoy the shady garden at *Binimel·là* restaurant (see p. 119). If you continue along the path to the coast, the beaches get grittier and turn red, and the cliffs are covered in a carpet of *socarells*. This native plant looks like soft moss from a distance, but if you inspect it more closely or even touch it, you'll discover that it's actually quite thorny.

If you feel like a swim on a secluded beach, then follow the coastal trail (no shade) from the western end of the bay to neighbouring ⚲ *Cala Pregonda*. It's about a 10-minute walk. The stunning cliffs look as if they've been carved by a sculptor, and the sea is so clear, you can always see the bottom. 🕮 *F2*

> **INSIDER TIP**
> **Nature's sculptures**

# PORT D'ADDAIA

🕮 *H3* **The bay winds its way inland like a river, thus providing natural protection to one of the few harbours on Menorca's north coast.**

The slopes of the inlet are covered with evergreen bushes and the landscape has a sedate quality into which the resort's unobtrusive buildings are harmoniously integrated. And the little marina on the eastern side of the "fjord" is also wonderfully tranquil. On the western side, you'll find the fishing harbour next to the *Na Macaret* resort. But just a few kilometres further east (up to the Cap de Favàritx), the landscape paints a very different and more dramatic picture: over millennia, the wind and sea have shaped the black shale into bizarre forms.

## EATING & DRINKING

### CORNER CAFÉ BAR

English name, Mediterranean cuisine and much more than just a bar: Choose several different tapas to get a taste of Chef Pere's distinctive style or just order a seafood *fideuà* (paella with pasta). The shady terrace with wicker chairs has a lovely ambience. Live music on Saturday afternoons. *Daily | Av. Port d'Addaia Local 4 | tel. 609 00 45 21 | €€*

## SPORT & ACTIVITIES

### DIVING & SNORKELLING

The perfect diving area is on your doorstep: the harbour diving centre *Blue Dive Menorca (daily 8am–8pm | Zona Comercial Port d'Addaia | tel. 971 94 02 51 | blue divemenorca.com)* offers a wide range of dives, from a snorkel safari (40 euros) to scuba-diving courses. The seashore here (and the little islands of Addaia and Cala Macaret) are a conservation area so they're a great place to spot many sea creatures.

# AROUND PORT D'ADDAIA

## ▟ CAP DE FAVÀRITX ★

*19km southeast of Port d'Addaia / 27 mins (by car on the Me-7 and Ctra de Favàritx/Cf-1)*

This is where Menorca's dark side emerges, wild and rugged. The little road ends at a black-and-white-striped lighthouse. As far as the eye can see there are slate stacks which glimmer in the sun. It's a wonderful place.

## ▤ CALA DE SA TORRETA ✦

*15km southeast of Port d'Addaia / 25 mins (by car on the Me-7)*

If you're looking for a secluded beach, then park your car in the village of Es Grau – on the small bridge over the La Gola canal – and follow the marked *Camí de Cavalls* to the north. Even before you crest the first rise, you'll see an unspoiled bay 3km ahead – it takes its name from a tower *(torreta)*. After another half hour, you'll reach the Cala de Sa Torreta. ⌀ J4

## ▥ S'ALBUFERA DES GRAU ★

*20km southeast of Port d'Addaia to the visitor centre / 19 mins (by car on the Me-9 and Me-7)*

This saltwater lagoon separated from the sea by a narrow dam is surrounded

Hiking, swimming, sailing: outdoor fun at S'Albufera des Grau National Park

by endless forest and flowering meadows. At 34.4km², S'Albufera des Grau is the second-largest wetland area on the Balearic Islands (the largest is on Mallorca). It is also the heart of the Unesco Biosphere Reservation. The coastline here is protected too and the beach is always covered in interesting seaweeds. Animals can live here undisturbed and many bird species nest on the shores of the shallow water, including ospreys and herons. The saltwater lagoon is full of wriggling eels and paddling turtles.

Visitors are allowed to hike through the nature reserve. A wooden walkway leads across marshes, and marked trails wind their way up to viewpoints. Shortly before you enter *Es Grau* (see below) – which has plenty of restaurants – there is a hut with information about the hiking trails. This is the starting point for the 🐾 free tour offered by the rangers (in Spanish only) and lasting two hours and 30 minutes. Tour groups are limited to 20 people, so make sure you register in advance by phone. If you want to walk a short stretch by yourself, follow signs to *Mirador*, a viewpoint high above the lake that you can reach in 15 minutes (one way). At the visitor centre, *Centre de Recepció Rodríguez Femenias* (Tue–Thu 9am–5pm, Fri–Sun 9am–3pm | admission free | Ctra Maó–Es Grau, Me-9, Km3.5, turn-off "Llimpa" | southeast of Fornells | tel. 971 17 77 05), a little further north, you can learn about the flora and fauna of the marshlands.

**INSIDER TIP**
**Explore a laguna landscape**

## 🟦7 ES GRAU

*22.3km southeast of Port d'Addaia / 21 mins (by car on the Me-7 and Me-5)*

This small fishing port is becoming a more and more popular destination for Menorcans and the narrow street and port bars are very busy, especially at weekends. Fine sand, a gently sloping beach, protected from the wind and waves by the island of Colom, and an almost perfect semi-circular shape are what define Es Grau's beach. However, in summer the bay throngs with pleasure boats. *Menorca en Kayak (C/ S'Arribada 8 | menorcaenkayak.com)* offer kayak courses and excursions. Once you have done their course you can also hire boats and set off on your own. You'll find decent basic food at *Bar Es Grau* (see p. 123). 🔲 *J4–5*

## 🟦8 ILLA D'EN COLOM

*22.8km southeast of Port d'Addaia / 36 mins (by car on the Me-7 and Me-5 to Es Grau, then by boat)*

This little island off the eastern coast is a natural paradise with rugged cliffs, seabirds, reptiles, secluded bays and two beaches. In summer a ferry *(departure from the port in Es Grau, Moll d'es Magatzems | 4 times daily | FB: BarcaColom)* makes the 500-m crossing and will take you to beautiful nearby bays. 🔲 *J4*

## 🟦9 ARENAL D'EN CASTELL ✈

*3km northwest of Port d'Addaia / 5 mins (by car on the Me-9 and C/ de Sa Marina)*

It's no wonder that a holiday resort

was built on this stunning, semi-circular bay. The long, gently sloping beach is one of the island's most beautiful, surrounded by green cliffs and crystal-clear sea. *H3*

### 🔟 ARENAL DE SON SAURA
*9.6km northwest of Port d'Addaia / 14 mins (by car on the Me-7)*
This mall holiday resort has a clean, white, semi-circular sandy beach. There is a simple restaurant, water-skiing, surfing and pedalo hire. If you want a bit more peace and quiet, then you can take the path (about 1.2km) at the left end of the beach to the next small cove, *Cala Pudent.*

# ES MERCADAL

*F4* **This little town (pop. 5,400) in the centre of the island is a popular stop on the way to Menorca's highest mountain. Enjoy a stroll through the wide streets, past the little white houses and through the markets.**

This is where they make the legendary *avarques* – simple but stylish sandals with soles made of tyres and leather heel straps. Most Menorcans know the town as a kind of culinary mecca. Its restaurants are famous for holding family parties. And there are lots of famous bakeries too.

## EATING & DRINKING

### MOLÍ DES RACÓ
In spite of its simple furnishings this is a good recommendation if you're looking for some authentic Menorcan cuisine. It's a lovely, 300-year-old mill with a relaxed ambience. 🦐 If you want to save money, order your meal to take away – It'll make for a great beach picnic! *Daily | C/ Major 53| tel. 971 37 53 92 | restaurantemoli desraco.com | €€*

## SHOPPING

Every Thursday you can meet crafts-people at the *Mercat Artesanal (7-10pm, in winter 6.30-9.30pm | Plaça del Pare Camps)*. A folk band plays music to dance to. If you're looking for the iconic Menorcan sandals, you can head for the *avarques* workshop *(Taller Gabriel Servera | Carrer Metges Camps 3)*. The well-known confectioner *Cas Sucrer (Sa Plaça | cassucrer.es)* makes excellent *turrón* (nougat) in varieties such as marzipan, ground peanuts, Turkish honey, chocolate or *amargos* (almond paste). To die for!

### CENTRE ARTESANAL DE MENORCA 🦐
This centre for craftspeople sells both trendy and traditional work. From cala-bash bottles to woven fabrics, pottery and ceramics, every piece is unique and you can watch the craftspeople at work. There is also a museum for Menorcan arts and crafts. *Mon–Fri 11am–2pm and 5–8pm, Sat 11am–2pm; March/April morning only; Nov–Feb closed | free admission | Av. del Metge Camps | Es Mercadal | tel. 971 15 36 44 | artesaniademenorca.com*

Where should we go next? Stroll through the Es Mercadal evening market

# AROUND ES MERCADAL

### 11 MONTE TORO ★

*5.5km east of Es Mercadal / 10 mins (by car on the Me-13)*

Like a hedgehog with radio antennae for spines, the 357m Monte Toro *(El Toro)* rises out of the somewhat hilly landscape. The island's highest point offers not only a fantastic view of Tramuntana to the north and Migjorn to the south but is also a point of orientation for the fishermen at sea; it is also responsible for much of Menorca's TV reception. At the eastern entrance of Es Mercadal a road branches off to Monte Toro.

Today it is mainly holidaymakers who make the pilgrimage to the *Monte*, as it is known to the Menorcans. The 17th-century *Mare de Deu del Toro* chapel nestles between the transmitter masts. In a vault next to the chapel, Franciscan nuns sell religious souvenirs, books and postcards. The *convent restaurant Sa Posada del Toro (closed in the evening | tel. 971 37 51 74 | saposadadeltoro.com | €)* serves good Menorcan food and has an affordable lunch menu. *G4*

**WHERE TO STAY IN TRAMUNTANA & THE NORTH**

**FUN FOR ALL THE FAMILY**

The *Carema Club Resort (193 Ap. | Urb. Playas de Fornells | Cala Tirant | tel. 971 15 42 18 | caremahotels.com | €€ | G2)* is mainly for families. It has large apartments and a "Splash Park" (not just for kids), and there's a nice beach on the doorstep too.

# MIGJORN, CENTRE & THE SOUTH

## THE ISLAND'S SPINE & AMAZING BEACHES

The north of the island is black, red and brown, the coast wild and rugged. Central and southern Menorca is completely different. The middle of the island is full of gently rolling hills covered in meadows and forests. Arable farming produces wonderful aubergines, artichokes and tomatoes.

Large ravines *(barrancs)* cut deep into the hilly landscape. Their lush greenery has earned them the name "the gardens of Menorca."

White, green, blue and turquoise: the stunning colours of Cala Mitjana

There are beautiful bays with white beaches and spectacular cliffs between them.

It's no wonder that some of the island's most popular resorts are in the south's mild climes – such as Cala Galdana, the long beaches at Sant Tomàs/Son Bou and the tranquil cove of Cala Trebalúger. Seawater shimmers azure above white limestone – it all looks like something straight out of a brochure!

# MIGJORN, CENTRE & THE SOUTH

**7** Binissues

ESPAÑA

Me-1

**8** Hort de Sant Patrici

Me-1

**Ferreries p.82**

Son Martorellet **4**

7km, 12 mins

Me-20

Me-22

11km, 15 mins

**Es Migjorn Gran**
p.85

**5** Cala Galdana ★

**6** Cala Mitjana ★

Cala Santa Galdana

Cala Mitjana

**9** Cova dels Coloms

Me-18

p.87
**Sant Tomàs**

Platja Sant Tomàs

25km, 27 mins

Platges de Son Bou

*Mar Mediterrània*

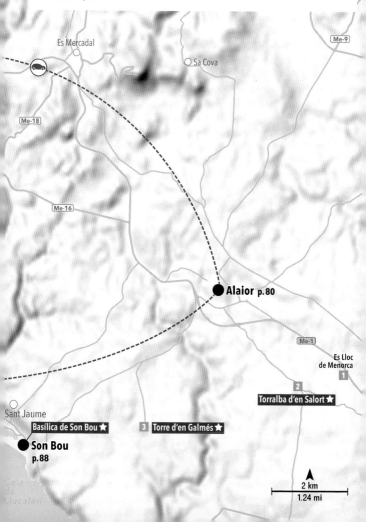

# MARCO POLO HIGHLIGHTS

★ **TORRALBA D'EN SALORT**
The most beautiful and best-preserved *taula* on Menorca ➤ p. 82

★ **TORRE D'EN GALMÉS**
A complete town was created from three *talaiots* and a *taula* sanctuary ➤ p. 82

★ **CALA GALDANA**
A picturesque bay surrounded by tree-lined cliffs ➤ p. 84

★ **CALA MITJANA**
White sand, bright blue sea. A great place for a dip ➤ p. 85

★ **BASÍLICA DE SON BOU**
Mysterious ruins on the beach – relics of an early Christian basilica ➤ p. 88

Es Mercadal

Sa Cova

Me-9

Me-18

Me-16

**Alaior** p. 80

Me-1

Es Lloc
de Menorca **1**

Sant Jaume

**2**
Torralba d'en Salort ★

Basílica de Son Bou ★

**3** Torre d'en Galmés ★

● **Son Bou**
p. 88

Cala
de
Llucalari

2 km
1.24 mi

# ALAIOR

📖 *G5* **White houses stacked on a hilltop overlooked by a church, and small cobbled streets just waiting to be explored. Founded in 1304, Alaior (pronounced: *aló*) is Menorca's most unspoilt, undiscovered and authentic spot.**

The town (pop. 9,400) is Menorca's third biggest and is home not just to the island's university but also its famous cheese. Menorcan cheese with the *Queso Maó* designation of origin comes from over 10,000 cows reared by around 100 dairy farmers. In addition to cows and cheese, a shoe factory is central to Alaior's economy alongside a number of family-run jewellery businesses.

SIGHTSEEING

### CAPELLA DE GRACIA

This small 16th-century chapel has pretty colonnades and is home to the tourist information office – a good place to start your visit. *July–Sept Mon–Sat 10.30am–1.30pm, 6–9pm | Coll del Palmer s/n | ⏱ 10 mins*

### CONVENT SANT DIEGO & PATI DE SA LLUNA

Once a Franciscan church built in 1629 during Alaior's golden age, this white cuboid with a belltower is today a small museum. The attached cloisters, *Pati de Sa Lluna*, are well worth exploring too. *Irregular opening hours | free admission | Carrer de Sant Diego s/n | ⏱ 15 mins*

### ERMITA SANT PERE NOU & CEMENTIRI

Another church on a hill. The Camí del Cos begins nearby and every year horse races take place there during celebrations in honour of the local patron saint (second weekend in August). Menorca's prettiest cemetery is just a few metres down the road. Huge mausoleums are surrounded by cypress and palm trees, and bougainvillea. *Irregular opening hours | Camí del Cos s/n | ⏱ 20 mins*

### ESGLÉSIA DE SANTA EULÀLIA

The imposing baroque façade of Santa Eulàlia (1301) towers above the little white houses of Alaior. You enter through a side door and emerge into a dark interior at the middle of which sits the eye-catching gold inlaid altar. *Irregular opening hours | Carrer des Retxats | ⏱ 15 mins*

## EATING & DRINKING

### ES FESTUC

More of a traditional tapas bar than a restaurant, but the food is prepared with love. They make a delicious beetroot hummus *(hummus de remolacha)*, cheese with pesto and wonderful desserts. *Daily 7am–midnight | C/ Es Carrero 38 | tel. 971 37 93 82 | FB: esfestuc | €*

## SHOPPING

On Wednesday evenings (7–11pm) during the summer, there is an arts and

**INSIDER TIP**
**Evening browsing**

The picturesque university town of Alaior is the centre for cheese-making on the island

crafts market with lots of regional food to try, as well as folk music and workshops. You can pick up stylish shoes at *Pons Quintana (Centro Comercial Balearica | C/ Sant Antoni 120 | ponsquintana.com)* and also at the *Gomila Melia shoe factory S.A. (C/ Miguel de Cervantes 46 | gomila.es).*

Sample and buy the famous cheese at *Coniga (Ctra Nova Parc 78 | coniga. com)* or at *La Payesa (Pons Martín | C/ Es Banyer 64 | lapayesa.es).*

# AROUND ALAIOR

### 1 ES LLOC DE MENORCA
*5km southeast from Alaior / 9 mins (by car on the ME-1)*

This well-designed zoo keeps kangaroos, emus, monkeys and lemurs in specially designed enclosures (you can go into some). The falconry show is also great and very informative. *March–Nov daily 10am–4pm | admission 13 euros, children (3-12 years) 8.50 euros (under 3s free) | Ctra General, Km7.8 | llocdemenorca.com*

## 2 TORRALBA D'EN SALORT ★

*5km south of Alaior / 10 mins (by car on the Ctra Alaior-Cala en Porter)*

This *talaiot* settlement from around 1000 BCE is now an archaeological park. The *Sa Taula de Torralba* shrine is especially interesting. It's an enormous T-shaped "table" in the middle of a pagan worship site and is one of the best preserved on the island. Animal bones and a small bronze figure of a bull were found near the circle of megaliths. During the full moon, night tours are available *(10 euros)* when the *taula* is bathed in mystical illumination. *June–Oct Tue–Sat 10am–8pm, Sun/Mon 10am–1pm; Nov–May Mon–Sat 10am–1pm, 3–6pm | admission 4 euros | ⊙ 30 mins | ▥ G5*

**INSIDER TIP**
**Prehistoric light show**

## 3 TORRE D'EN GALMÉS ★ ⚑

*7km southwest of Alaior / 13 mins (by car on the Ctra de Son Bou, dirt track after 2.5km)*

One of the most impressive sights on the island is this prehistoric town. Three *talaiots* and a *taula* sanctuary formed a settlement around 1400 BCE, of which the remains of rooms, defensive walls, cisterns, caves and storage chambers are still visible. A burial chamber and a hall (probably used as a store or for gatherings) are situated a little away from the other remains. *Mon–Sat 10am–2pm, 4–8pm, Sun 10am–2pm | admission 4 euros, free on Mon; free admission March–Nov but info centre closed | ⊙ 1 hr | ▥ G5–6*

# FERRERIES

▥ E4 **With its rust-red cliffs, reddish brown fields and a newer part of the town near the main road which is certainly not a thing of beauty, the town of Ferreries (pop. 4,600) is, at first glance, a bit off-putting.**

However, an atmospheric old town in the upper area more than compensates for those first negative impressions. Carrer de Sa Font has plenty of places which exude historical charm.

## SIGHTSEEING

### CENTRE DE GEOLOGÍA DE MENORCA 🐵 🐀

"Discover Menorca by its colours" is the motto of this small museum which shows where all the red, black, white and ochre rocks on the island come from. *May–Sept Tue–Sun 10am–2pm, 6–8pm; Oct/Nov and March/April Tue–Sat 10am–2pm | free admission | C/ Mallorca 2 | geologiamenorca.com*

## EATING & DRINKING

### LIORNA

An idiosyncratic mix of art and dining with changing menus and exhibitions. The pizzas are good. If you are looking for a creative atmosphere and are willing to overlook waiters' errors, then this is the place for you. *Daily 8–11pm | C/ de Dalt 9 | tel. 971 37 39 12 | €€€*

### MESÓN EL GALLO

The traditional pub's charming vine-bedecked pergola and large portions of first-class grilled meat attract Menorcans from all over the island. *April–Oct Tue–Sun 1.30–3pm, 7.30–11pm | Ctra Cala Galdana Km1.5 | tel. 971 37 30 39 | mesonelgallo.com | €€*

**INSIDER TIP**
**Rural meat fest**

## SHOPPING

The *Mercat de Nit,* a popular Friday market in the centre *(July/Aug 7–11pm),* sells fruit, vegetables, hams and cheese. There is another craft market on Saturday morning. You really must try the local *bunyols de fromatge* – dough fritters fried in oil with a cheese filling – from a bakery in the old town. The goldsmith *Núria Deyà (C/ Ciutadella 12a | tel. 971 37 35 23 | nuriadeya.com)* makes lovely jewellery with floral designs and simple shapes in her small workshop.

**INSIDER TIP**
**Deliciously greasy**

### CALZADOS RIA S.L.

*Avarques,* the typical Menorcan sandals, have been made here since 1947. Their straps are made from leather and the soles from car tyres. Showroom next door. *C/ Trencadors 25 | tel. 971 37 30 70 | ria.es*

Horse parade in Ferreries

# AROUND FERRERIES

### 🏇 SON MARTORELLET 🏇

*3.2km southwest of Ferreries / 6 mins (by car on the Me-22)*

Horsey people make pilgrimages to this estate which puts on amazing four-legged spectacles with their "Dancing and Dreaming Horses". During the day you can also visit the stables. *Stables Mon, Thu/Fri 5–7pm, admission 6.50 euros, children 3.40 euros | evening shows June–Sept, Tue and Thu 8.30pm | admission from 35.50 euros, children from 18.50 euros; tickets also online | Ctra Cala Galdana, Km1.7 | tel. 971 37 34 06 | sonmartorellet.com | ▱ E4*

A cheese-and-wine tasting in the beautiful surroundings of the Hort de Sant Patrici

### 5 CALA GALDANA ★ ⚤

*8.5km southwest of Ferreries / 9 mins (by car on the Me-22)*

At one time this green oasis, surrounded by dark grey coastal cliffs, was described as "picturesque" or "like paradise". Unfortunately, its charm is now being buried under concrete as the *Cala Galdana* resort continues to expand westwards across the bay. As you arrive and pass the first hotel (turn off to the left), you will be able to see the whole place. The beach is a good 500m of golden sand, making it ideal for families with small children. The sea in the bay only becomes rough with a southerly wind, which is rare. The restaurant *El Mirador* (daily | tel. 971 15 45 03 | elmirador-restaurante.com | €€€) has a fantastic location carved into the rock on a peninsula off the coast. But don't expect too much from the kitchen.

The enormous hotel *Meliá Cala Galdana* might be a bit of an eyesore but the view from its *Beach Club El Cape Nao (closed Oct–April | €€)* is the best here. It's open to non-guests too.

Motor boats, dinghies and kayaks for the whole family are available at *Sports Nautics (May–Oct | on the beach | tel. 676 99 12 44|)*. Several times a week, excursion boats set sail from Cala Galdana and head along the south coast.

One provider is *Menorca en Barco (mobile tel. 605 49 29 93 | menorca enbarcom)*. An alternative is the water taxi from *Menorca Taximar (May–Oct daily 9am–2pm every hour from Cala Galdana | 25 euros per person return | menorcataximar.com)*.

It stops at half a dozen secluded beaches (and grottoes), and you can decide which *playa* you'd like to spend the next few hours basking on. You will be picked up at a fixed time and ferried back to your starting point. *D5*

**INSIDER TIP**
**Bay watch**

## 6 CALA MITJANA ★ ⚲

*9.5km southwest of Ferreries / 32 mins (by car on the Me-2 to Cala Galdana, then 20 mins' walk over the cliffs)*

The bay is often called "Spain's Caribbean" and lots of people think it is one of the most beautiful bays in the Mediterranean. Bright white sand leads into azure sea with pine-flecked cliffs around it – it's a wonderful spot for a day out with a picnic. Follow the path further east to the lovely, quiet ⚑ *Cala Trebalúger* (40 mins, some tricky sections).

Lots of caves and prehistoric remains sit among the ravines, which later feed into Cala Trebalúger. Roughly halfway between Cala Galdana and Cala Sant Tomás you will find two more, often deserted bays: *Cala Fustam*, a small beach with a backdrop of pine trees and a large cave at its left-hand edge, and *Cala Escorxada*. Both can only be reached via a difficult path along the coast. ⌖ *D5*

## 7 BINISSUES

*5.5km northwest of Ferreries / 9 mins (by car on the Me-1)*

Make yourself at home in the aristocratic Salort family's erstwhile estate and learn how the affluent upper-class once lived and how they made their money. In the outbuildings, there is a dairy, a sausage-making workshop, a bakery, and a threshing floor – join a tasting if you want to try the home-made products. Additionally, you can get an overview of Menorca's varied landscape in the little natural history museum, and at the restaurant *(€€)* you can enjoy Menorcan cuisine and a spectacular view of the hilly green landscape. *May–Oct Tue–Sun 10.30am–5pm, restaurant until 11pm | admission 7 euros | tel. 971 37 37 28 | binissues.com |* 🕐 *1 hr |* ⌖ *D3*

## 8 HORT DE SANT PATRICI

*1.9km north of Ferreries/4 mins (by car via Camí Sant Patrici)*

Set in Mediterranean gardens, it is hard to imagine a nicer setting to learn about (and try) local cheese than this estate. The creamery and cheese museum explain how some of Spain's best dairy products are produced. The delicatessen sells honey, home-made jams and hams. You can try local wines with the home-made cheese on a guided tour. *April–Oct Mon–Sat 9am–1pm, 3.30–7.30pm; Nov–Mar Mon–Fri 9am–1pm | admission free, guided tours (in Spanish: Tue, Fri 10am; in English Mon 10am. Register in advance) 8 euros | Camí de Sant Patrici | tel. 971 37 37 02 | sant patrici.com |* ⌖ *E4*

> **INSIDER TIP**
> **Perfect partners: cheese and wine**

# ES MIGJORN GRAN

⌖ *E–F5* **Es Migjorn Gran is really just a few houses on a hill, surrounded by fields with drystone walls coarsing between them.**

It is a good place to see what

Ocean spray and crashing surf: mountain biker near Sant Tomàs

Menorca used to be like: pretty but unspectacular, embedded in a charming landscape. At the heart of town, one-storey homes cower around the church (with its eye-catching blue dome). There are also a couple of excellent inns that make their livelihood from travellers heading toward the south coast.

## EATING & DRINKING

### S'ENGOLIDOR

Hearty, traditional Menorcan cuisine such as local pork ribs or stingray with capers served on a beautiful terrace with idyllic views. They have a few basic rooms for those who like the food (and wine) too much. *Closed Mon and at lunchtime | C/*

**INSIDER TIP**
**Seafood with a sting**

*Major 3 | tel. 971 37 01 93 | sengolidor. com | €*

# AROUND ES MIGJORN GRAN

### 🔟 COVA DELS COLOMS
*3km southwest of Es Migjorn Gran / 8 mins (by car on the Me-18, then walk)*

Locals call this cave – which is only accessible on foot (see p. 114, "Walk to Cova dels Coloms) – "the cathedral" because of its considerable size (24m high, 110m long and 16m wide). Recent research revealed it was a sacred site in pre-Christian times.

joined up to create a settlement which was clearly used as a dwelling.
*Ⅲ E5*

# SANT TOMÀS

*Ⅲ E5* **Of all the resorts on the southern coast, Sant Tomàs might be the most beautiful. Here, you have access to multiple playas that are only separated from one another by rocky outcrops.**

Beyond the village's 530-m-long beach, there is a line of protected, pine-dotted dunes, at whose feet rare sand lilies grow. A promenade runs beyond the trees, behind which "hide" a few squat hotels. There are also two or three rows of villas with lush gardens.

According to an old Menorcan superstition, couples who enter the cave together will separate after a short time; people who meet independently of one another in the cave, however, will be united by the power of fate.

On the way from Es Migjorn Gran down to Sant Tomàs beach there are three archaeological sites. The *Talaiot de Binicudrell* has not yet been excavated but work is planned. The prehistoric settlement of *Sant Agustí Vell* is well known for a large stone building covered with beams which led earlier generations of archaeologists to the conclusion, now outdated, that the *taules* were only central supports for larger buildings. The third settlement, *Santa Mónica*, is interesting because a row of *navetas* (precursors of the *talaiots*) here were

## EATING & DRINKING

### ES BRUC
On the western edge of Sant Tomàs, you can sit by the seaside and enjoy delicious seafood. The amazing view may make you forget your food! *Daily* | *Sant Tomás–Sant Adeodat* | *tel. 971 37 04 88* | *€–€€*

> **INSIDER TIP**
> Don't forget to chew

### ES PINS
This beach restaurant is decked out in white and tucked between the pines on the eastern edge of Sant Tomàs. Menorcan cuisine, sea views and lots of loungers. *Daily* | *tel. 971 37 05 41* | *€–€€*

## SPORT & ACTIVITIES

can hire kayaks, SUP boards and paddleboats at the beach *(sportskayak.es)*.

## BEACHES

The makings of a perfect holiday: soft, white sand which stretches out in both directions. San Tomás's beach slopes so seamlessly down to the sea that you hardly notice when you are in the water. The beach is at its widest near the village and there are lifeguards. Further west the wilder *Sant Adeodat* beach seamlessly merges into *Binigaus* beach. The 1.2-km-long coastal path runs along the foot of low sandstone cliffs pockmarked with caves. The caves provide some shade and is probably the reason the beach is popular with nudists. Further to the west are the bays of *Cala Escorxada* and *Cala Fustam*, which are only accessible on foot (or by boat). At the eastern end of Sant Tomàs, you can take an attractive coastal path first to the Platja de Atalis, then to the dunes and wetlands of Son Bou, which connect to the long sandy beach *Platges de Son Bou*.

# SON BOU

*F5-6* **At 4km, the Platges de Son Bou are the longest sandy beaches on Menorca. Golden sand and a gentle slope into the sea make these beaches the ideal spot for families.**

Consequently, there was simply no way to stop big hotels moving in here. The first of these, the huge *Sol Milanos Pinguïnos*, was built on the beach in the 1970s. They stand in sharp contrast to the ruins of the ★ *Basílica de Son Bou*, an early Christian basilica from the fifth century on the eastern edge of the bay that wasn't discovered until 1951. Only the base of two rows of columns, the foundation walls and a font with a cloverleaf-shaped basin remain. It never gets busy (even in the high season) at the northern end of the beach where there are protected sand dunes.

## EATING & DRINKING

Enjoy a break from relaxing at the chilled *Xiringuito Es Corb Mari* beach bar *(May–Oct daily from 10am | Playa de Son Bou | near the Hotel Sol Milanos Pingüinos | tel. 717 70 64 34 | €–€€).* It's most beautiful at sunset,

**INSIDER TIP**
**You've earned a drink**

with a mojito in your hand. The seafood is also delicious, and the boss, Marino, gets a live band in every night. *Casa Andrés (daily | Centro Comercial Son Bou 39 | tel. 971 37 19 18 | €€)* may look like an ugly tourist trap from the outside but its large, delicious plates of fried fish will convince you otherwise.

### FORN DE TORRE SOLI NOU

Housed in a traditional Menorcan building with a spectacular terrace and a beautiful interior too. The meat dishes are excellent and the ice cream

Sand castles? Bollards? No, it's the ruins of an early Christian basilica in Son Bou

home-made. *Urb. Torre Soli Nou 28 | main road towards Son Bou | tel. 971 37 28 98 | esforntsn.com | €€*

## SPORT & ACTIVITIES

You can hire pedalos on the beach. 👣 Some even have small slides for kids!

### SON BOU SCUBA

At this diving school they are passionate about diving and offer courses for everyone, from beginners to advanced divers. They also run regular dives to explore shipwrecks and caves. Diving equipment also available to hire. *April–Oct | Centro Comercial San Jaime | mobile tel. 696 62 82 65 | sonbouscuba.com*

## WHERE TO STAY IN MIGJORN, CENTRE & THE SOUTH

### THE NATURAL WORLD

If you're looking for rural Menorca, *Binisaid (4 rooms | Ctra Ferreries–Cala Galdana, Km4.3 | tel. 971 15 50 63 | binisaid.com | €€ | ⌂ D5)* is the place for you. Located near the Cala Galdana in an amazing spot between two ravines and completely enveloped by forest, almost everything they serve at breakfast is home produced.

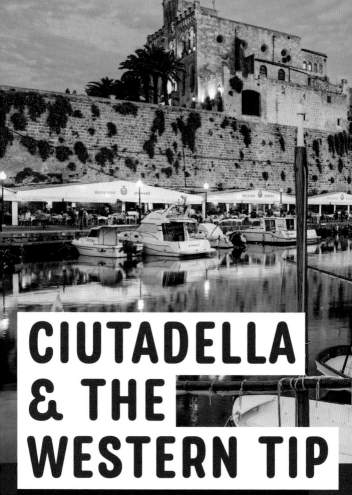

# CIUTADELLA & THE WESTERN TIP

## THE PRETTIEST TOWN & BEAUTIFUL BAYS

With its narrow alleyways and ochre-coloured buildings, Ciutadella's old town – built on a cliff over 2,000 years ago – radiates Mediterranean charm.

Wandering through its streets and taking breaks at cafés in the shade of its colonnades is a great way to spend a day. The many restaurants at the harbour give it a good buzz. Out at sea, the boats – including traditional Menorcan *llauts* – are packed together on their moorings.

Dine with a view of the harbour in Ciutadella

New resorts have sprung up around the city, such as Cala En Forcat in the west (popular with Brits) or the luxury resort of Cala Morell in the north and the constantly expanding Cala Blanca and Son Xoriguer in the south. But there is also plenty of wilderness, such as the cliffs at Cape Punta Nati in the north and the sensational undeveloped coves in the south: Son Saura, Cala en Turqueta and Cala Macarella.

# CIUTADELLA & THE WESTERN TIP

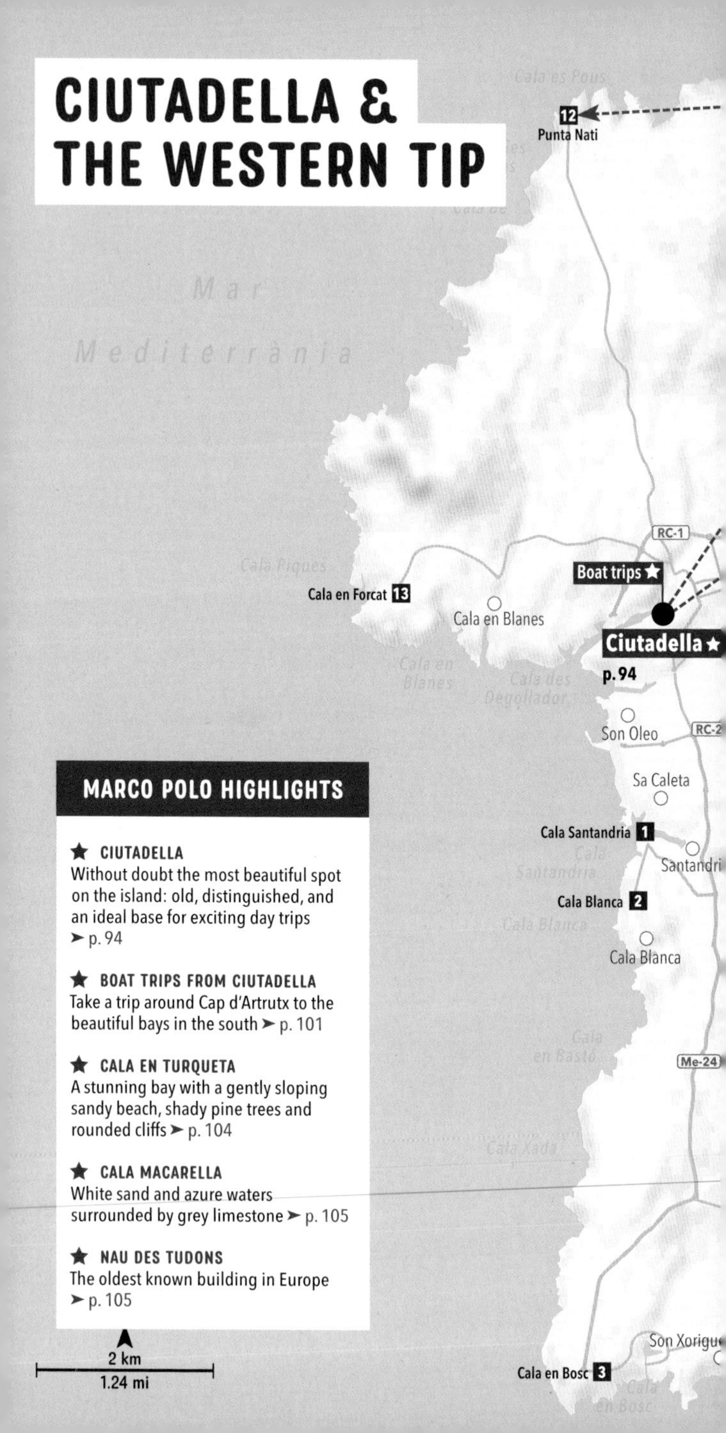

Mar
Mediterrània

**12**
Punta Nati

Cala en Forcat **13**

Cala en Blanes

**Boat trips ★**

RC-1

● **Ciutadella ★**
p. 94

Son Oleo

RC-2

Sa Caleta

**Cala Santandria 1**

Santandri

**Cala Blanca 2**

Cala Blanca

Me-24

Son Xorigu

**Cala en Bosc 3**

## MARCO POLO HIGHLIGHTS

★ **CIUTADELLA**
Without doubt the most beautiful spot on the island: old, distinguished, and an ideal base for exciting day trips ➤ p. 94

★ **BOAT TRIPS FROM CIUTADELLA**
Take a trip around Cap d'Artrutx to the beautiful bays in the south ➤ p. 101

★ **CALA EN TURQUETA**
A stunning bay with a gently sloping sandy beach, shady pine trees and rounded cliffs ➤ p. 104

★ **CALA MACARELLA**
White sand and azure waters surrounded by grey limestone ➤ p. 105

★ **NAU DES TUDONS**
The oldest known building in Europe ➤ p. 105

▲
2 km
1.24 mi

13km, 19 mins

**Cala Morell**
p. 107

Cala Algaiarens **14**

1 km, 19 mins

10km, 15 mins

12km, 22 mins

**15** Cavalls Son Àngel

Pedreres de S'Hostal
**11**

Me-1

**10**

**Nau des Tudons** ★

**9** Torre Llafuda

E S P A Ñ A

**8** Son Catlar

**7**
**Cala Macarella** ★

**6**
**Cala en Turqueta** ★

Cala de Son Saura **5**

Cala Parejals

# CIUTADELLA

(⟦ B3-4) **Although with 30,600 inhabitants ★ Ciutadella is a little bigger than Maó, life here is lived at a more leisurely pace than in its vibrant rival. People seem to have more time here than in the hustle and bustle of Maó.**

Days seem longer, the pace is more humane. When the barber runs out of customers in the afternoon, he will sun himself on a folding chair outside his shop. A stranger here is often greeted with a nod of the head and the older generation meets up for animated discussion in groups or in the shadow of the obelisk on the Plaça d'es Born.

The so-called "Little City" has had many rulers and many names over the centuries. First it was Iammo then Iamona, and then Medina Menorquina before settling on Ciutadella. A quick run-down of its rulers is helpful too – the Romans replaced the Carthaginians before they were usurped by the Vandals who fell to the Arabs. The Aragonese erased all traces of these latter "heathens" in 1287, pulling down their mosque and giving the city its present name. In the 16th and 17th century the town flourished once again. Churches and monasteries were established, the centre was enclosed by town walls and it became home to the island's diocese before assuming the role of Menorcan capital until the Brits ettled on Maó in 1722. It was only after the end Franco's dictatorship that

the island's council held a referendum to decide which of the two major towns should become the administrative centre of Menorca. Ciutadella only was defeated by a few votes.

## SIGHTSEEING

### CATEDRAL 🛐

The Carrer Major d'es Born leads to the cathedral on Plaça de la Catedral. It partly owes its massive, angular appearance to a reinforcement of the structure after part of the dome collapsed in 1628. In 1795 a papal edict elevated the new building to the status of Cathedral of Menorca, provoking considerable criticism from Maó. Today's bell tower is a reminder of the minaret of a mosque which dominated the square until the 13th century *(Mon–Sat 10am–4pm)*.

Countless anecdotes and legends surround the church. It is said that, when the new building was constructed, the window frames had to be sealed because hundreds of birds got into the church during prayers. In the course of history, the cathedral also became a place of refuge for many people who had fallen into disfavour with the island's governors. Sacred treasures are on exhibition in the vestry and chapter room, including a silver rosary Madonna. *Admission 4 euros, combined with the Església del Socors 6 euros | bisbatdemenorca.com | ⏱ 30 mins | ⟦ d4-5*

### PALAU OLIVAR 🏛

In Señor Luis de Oliver's palace you can saunter through noble halls

Ciutadella's port bay cuts deeply into the town like a fjord

adorned with frescos, including an unusual frieze with all the animals on Noah's ark. The palace has more the air of a private house than a museum. It feels as if you could move in, have a nap in one of the grand bedrooms, eat off the finest porcelain in the banqueting hall and watch the world go by outside. The entrance to the *judería*, the Jewish quarter, and its basic houses is near the palace *(Carrer Palau, Carrer Sant Jeroni and Carrer Sant Francesc)*. *Mon–Sat 10am–2pm | admission 4 euros, children under 12 free | Plaça de la Catedral 8 | ⏱ 30 mins. | ⊞ d4*

**INSIDER TIP**
**Just like home**

## PALAU SALORT

Would you like to live here? Stroll through the many rooms of this palace; they're full of antique furniture, heavy crystal chandeliers and brocade curtains. *Mon–Sat 10am–2pm | admission 3 euros | C/ Major d'es Born | ⊞ c–d4*

## ESGLÉSIA DEL ROSER

Carrer del Roser branches off to the south from opposite the *Porta de la Llum* (light gate), the entrance to the cathedral on the right. After 50 paces you come to the narrow façade of the *Església del Roser* (1664), which is home to an interesting gallery. *Admission free | ajciutadella.org | ⏱ 10 mins | ⊞ d5*

## ESGLÉSIA DEL SOCORS & MUSEU DIOCESÀ

Founded in 1648, this Augustinian monastery today houses the *Museu*

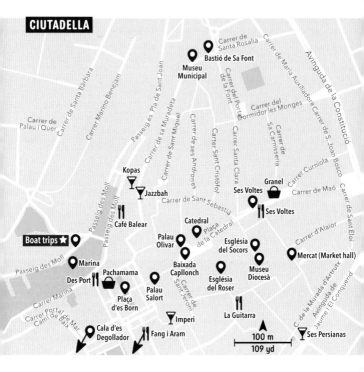

**CIUTADELLA**

Carrer de Santa Rosalia
Carrer de Maria Auxiliadora
Avinguda de la Constitució
Carrer de S. Joan Bosco
Bastió de Sa Font
Museu Municipal
Carrer de Santa Bárbara
Carrer Marino Benejam
Carrer de Palau i Quer
Passeig es Pla de Sant Joan
Carrer de sa Murada
Carrer del Portal de la Font
Carrer del Dormidor les Monges
Carrer de sa Carnisseria
Carrer de Sant Miquel
Carrer de ses Andrones
Carrer Sant Cristòfol
Carrer Santa Clara
Carrer Curniola
Kopas
Jazzbah
Carrer de Sant Sebastià
Granel
Ses Voltes
Ses Voltes
Carrer de Maó
Carrer de Sant Eloi
Passeig des Moll
Café Balear
Catedral
Plaça de la Catedral
Esglèsia del Socors
Carrer d'Alaior
Boat trips ★
Palau Olivar
Baixada Capllonch
Esglèsia del Socors
Mercat (Market hall)
Passeig des Moll
Marina
Pachamama
Baixada Capllonch
Esglèsia del Roser
Museu Diocesà
C. de la Murada d'Arrutx
Des Port
Plaça d'es Born
Palau Salort
Carrer de Sant Jeroni
Avinguda de Jaume El Conqueror
Carrer Marina
Carrer Portal de Baix
Camí de Mar
Cala d'es Degollador
Fang i Aram
Imperi
La Guitarra
Ses Persianas

100 m
109 yd

---

*Diocesà*, a museum exhibiting archaeological finds, taxidermy and paintings by local artists. The cloister and church are worth the visit alone. Classical concerts are held here as part of the summer *Festival Musica d'Estiu*. Mon–Sat 10am–4pm | admission 4 euros, 6 euros with the Catedral | C/ Seminari 7 | ⏱ 30 mins | 🗺 d5–6

**INSIDER TIP**
**Heavenly music**

## PLAÇA D'ES BORN

The obelisk on Plaça d'es Born is a reminder of the *Any de sa Desgracia* ("Year of Disaster"). It casts its shadow every morning on the *Ajuntament (town hall)* which was once an Arab fortress, then the castle of King Alfonso III who drove the Moors out and claimed the city and island for the crown. The present building dates back to the 19th century. Every year on 9 July a commemoration takes place on the square recalling the event when 15,000 "infidels" laid siege to the town in 1558. It also celebrates the heroes of Ciutadella who, for seven days, bravely defied the superior forces before the town fell and was almost totally destroyed. Behind the town hall, a viewing platform *(mirador)* on the *Bastió des Governador* (daily 9am–1pm), towers above the city walls (the view is worth the climb).

There are several cafés and restaurants on the lower floors of the *Palau Torresaura* and the *Palau Vivó*. All the buildings on the square were built using Marés, the distinctive breathable golden sandstone – a medieval air-conditioning system. *Talaia Cultura (mobile tel. 660 42 52 54 | talaiacultura.com)* run city tours (incl. the palaces).

To the north the square is bordered by the *Cercle Artístic* and the *Teatre Municipal d'es Born* (1881), the city theatre. Not much art happens in the "Artistic Circle", instead it is a place of loud debate. Films are shown in the theatre and it also holds concerts. There are great bars and the monastic chapel of *Sant Francesc* opposite. *c4*

## BAIXADA CAPLLONCH

The *Ca'n Squella* palace and the bishop's palace *Palau Episcopal* (both 17th century) are situated on the edge of Carrer Sant Sebastia and Carrer del Bisbé. In the quiet streets the aroma of fresh bread still wafts from many a bakery in the morning. Further to the west the steps of *Baixada Capllonch* come into view leading down to the sea. They are lined with souvenir stalls and shops. The popular *Café Balear* (see p. 99) is around the corner on the right. *d4*

## MARINA

Ciutadella's port is split down the middle. From the right bank, boats set off to take people on trips along the south coast, while on the left, there are

The town hall on Plaça d'es Born stands on the site of an earlier Arab fortress

Pots on display in the Museu Municipal were made a long, long time ago

exclusive restaurants, serving fresh fish to well-heeled guests. *□□ c3–4*

## SES VOLTES

Ses Voltes is the name of the arcades which line both sides of *Carrer Josep M Ouadrado*. Shops and restaurants thrive in the shade of the arches, each with its own charm. The bars on the adjoining *Plaça Nova* are normally busy. Straight ahead you come to *Plaça Alfons III* – or *Plaça de Ses Palmeres*, as the townspeople call it – and from there to *Camí de Maó* which crosses the island up to the east coast. To the west is *Carrer de Sant Antoni*, then *Carrer de Sant Josep*. Here you will find restaurants and cafés mostly frequented by locals. To the right at the end of *Carrer de Santa Clara* you come to the palace of the Baron of Lluriach *(Castell Lluriach)*, the first

nobleman on Menorca, appointed by Charles II after the battle with the Arab occupiers on Spain's south coast.

## MERCAT (MARKET HALL) 🏳

The sun only penetrates the small, quiet alleys around the market hall at about midday. Nevertheless, Mediterranean ambience reigns supreme at the *Mercat* (market). In the white and dark grey tiled building each guild takes up one side. For example, the butchers look out over the Carrer de la Palma with its series of vegetable stalls and traditional market bars. One of these 🍴 Ulises (*Mon–Fri 7am–14.30pm, 7–11pm, Sat 7.30am–3pm | Plaça Mercat | tel. 971 38 00 31 | €)* will charge around 2-4 euros to cook the fish you buy from the market stalls which

> **INSIDER TIP**
> Bring your own fish

you can then eat in some of the best seats in the arcades. The breakfast and daily specials are good value too. *ᗯ d-e6*

## BASTIO DE SA FONT & MUSEU MUNICIPAL

The original fortress from the 14th century was destroyed in 1558 by the Turks and not rebuilt until the end of the 17th century. Today, *Bastió de Sa Font* houses the *Museu Municipal*. It documents Menorca's chequered history from prehistory to the present using historical documents, archaeological finds and other artefacts. *Tue–Sat 10am–2.30pm, May–Sept also 6–9pm | admission 2.46 euros (Wed free) / Plaça de Sa Font 15 | ⏱ 30 mins | ᗯ f3–4*

## CALA D'ES DEGOLLADOR

If you're planning to spend a bit more time in Ciutadella, it's worth taking a stroll southward from the fishing and boating harbour along the fjord-like bay *(Carrer Marina/Camí de Boix)*. First, you'll pass beautiful villas, then the octagonal guard tower of *Castell de Sant Nicolau (Tue–Sat 10am–1pm | free admission)* and old fortresses that have sunk halfway into the sea. After about 500m, you'll reach the smaller fjord Cala d'es Degollador, which owes its gruesome name ("Cutthroat Bay") to a pirate raid many, many years ago. There is a tiny beach halfway along the bay although it's more fun to slip into the turquoise water from the smooth rocks. *ᗯ B4*

**INSIDER TIP**
**Swim in the pirates' bay**

## EATING & DRINKING

### CAFÉ BALEAR

Popular tapas and seafood stop for tourists and locals alike. The small restaurant has become an island institution with its good lunch menu and delicious seafood specialities. *Daily in the high season | Pla de Sant Joan 12 | tel. 971 38 00 05 | cafebalear.com | €€–€€€ | ᗯ d3–4*

### DES PORT

From this blue and white restaurant on the harbour, you can gaze out over the fishing boats while enjoying delicious Menorcan cuisine prepared by the owner, Tolo. Why not try his salad with local cheese and tomato chutney followed by sea bream with rocket or tender lamb filet on a bed of sliced potatoes? The large rock cave provides perfect shelter in bad weather. *Daily | C/ de Marina 23 | tel. 971 48 00 22 | €€ | ᗯ c4*

**INSIDER TIP**
**A cosy cave**

### FANG I ARAM

The only vegetarian restaurant for miles offers delightfully created menus which can be vegan or gluten free on request *(lunchtime Mon–Fri just 13 euros)* and breakfast four days a week *(Mon–Thu 10.30am–noon)*. With comfy sofas and a reading area, it is cosy and laid-back. *Closed Sun | C/ Gabriel Martí i Bella 11 | tel. 971 38 48 71 | restaurantevegetariano menorca.com | €–€€ | ᗯ 0*

A landmark in Ciutadella's old town – the restaurant Ses Voltes

### LA GUITARRA

Gabriel and Izaskun serve tasty and traditional Balearic cuisine in their lively cellar or out on the terrace. Their specialities include *frito marinero* (fried seafood), *bacalao* (cod with a honey and aioli crust) and *tumbet* (stewed vegetables). The home-made mascarpone ice cream is the icing on the cake. *Closed Sun | C/ Dolores 1 | tel. 971 38 13 55 | €€*

**INSIDER TIP** Balearic bites

### SES VOLTES

Always busy from morning to night. A filling sandwich for breakfast, a snack for lunch and haute cuisine in the evening – this restaurant celebrates the best of what Menorcan cuisine has to offer. Housed in a three-storey town house at the heart of Ciutadella, the restaurant serves tapas on the ground floor and à la carte menu upstairs. Stylish and relaxed. *C/ Ses Voltes 16–22 | tel. 971 38 14 98 | recibaria.com | €–€€€| ⅏ d5*

## SHOPPING

In the summer, artists and artisans sell their wares on *Baixada Capllonch*, the steps going down to the port.

### GRANEL

A cathedral to fine food, Ciutadella's best delicatessen sells a wide assortment of island goodies such as cheeses, salami, ham, sweet pastries, jams, honey, liqueurs, wine, gin, dried herbs, etc. You can also try before you buy. *Ses Voltes 8 | granel.cat | ⅏ e5*

## PACHAMAMA

Clothing, glam jewellery and cool accessories. *Plaça d'es Born 27–28 | ⌐ c4–5*

## SPORT & ACTIVITIES

⭐ *Boat trips* with *Rutas Marítimas de la Cruz* take you to remote beaches and bays which are otherwise not accessible. The little boat travels along sections of the western and southern coast, past *Cala de Son Saura, Cala en Turqueta* and *Cala Macarella* to *Cala Galdana*. It stops twice for swimming breaks in attractive bays, and you get a meal of paella with sangria or lemonade on board too. The journey starts at the old harbour in Ciutadella *(June– Sept daily 10am)*; you should arrive at the harbour by 9.30am to secure your place. The return trip leaves at 5pm. *Ticket are available at the harbour ticket office (49 euros) or online (44 euros) | Port Antic, Pantalán 1 | tel. 971 48 14 12 | rutasmaritimasdelacruz. com | ⌐ d3*

## COOKERY COURSE

You can learn how to make a delicious seafood stew or the distinctive *arroz caldoso* with its red prawns at *Cuk-Cuk* restaurant *(Tue–Sat 12.30–3.30pm and Mon–Sat 7–11pm | C/ de Sant Pere Alcantara 13 | tel. 971 38 07 03 | cuk-cuk.com)* in the old town. Reservations are necessary and, depending on the dish, the courses cost 28–36 euros incl. a drink and dessert *(duration 1–2 hrs)*.

## CYCLING

If you want to hire bikes for longer than a couple of days, *Velos Joan (C/ Sant Isidre 32–34 | tel. 971 38 15 76 | velosjoan.com | ⌐ c6)* is your best bet.

## DIVING

The western tip of Menorca has rich and varied marine life and a wide range of diving centres. One well-established *PADI diving centre (Cala en Busquets 10 | Edificio Las Terrazas | tel. 696 90 31 60 | scubaplus.org)* is right next to the entrance to Ciutadella's port. It offers training, equipment hire and guided dives.

## TENNIS

*Club de Tenis Ciutadella (Torre del Ram | tel. 971 38 84 56 | clubtenis ciutadella.com)* has public courts with floodlights meaning you can still play after the heat of the day.

## BEACHES

The *Cala d'es Degollador* is a small, pretty bay at the southern edge of the city (near the *Port Ciutadella* hotel). Locals tend to go to *Cala Algaiarens* (see p. 108) or *Cala Son Saura* to swim.

## WELLNESS

Some of Ciutadella's hotels let non-guests use their spa facilities. Housed in a 16th-century building, the spa in the five-star *Can Faustino (Carrer de sa Muradeta 22 | tel. 971 48 91 91 | canfaustino.com)* is particularly nice, with an indoor pool and professional treatments.

## NIGHTLIFE

Ciutadella is Menorca's nightlife hot-spot – and is particularly lively on Saturdays. Flyers are handed out during the week advertising free entry (usually only for women) or a free drink.

### IMPERI

"See and be seen" is the motto in this popular, traditional bar where they serve hearty *llonguet* – Menorcan sandwiches – with the drinks. *Plaça d'es Born 7 | ⊞ c4*

### JAZZBAH

The bars on *Es Pla de Sant Joan*, the road down to the harbour, are particularly popular these days. Fishermen used to haul their boats up here to paint them in the shade of the warehouses, but today it is a blaze of neon. *Jazzbah*, one of the city's oldest clubs, is enjoying its new status as the cool hang-out. There's a "cheesy" floor downstairs and a large terrace upstairs where you can relax with a cocktail or beer. *Port de Ciutadella | Es Pla de Sant Joan 3 | jazzbah.es | ⊞ e3–4*

### KOPAS

There's a different theme on each storey and they alternate between dance floors and chill-out zones. It is worth going up to the very top for the amazing views across Es Pla. There are also regular live events. *Es Pla de Sant Joan s/n | kopasclub.com | ⊞ e4*

### SES PERSIANAS

Locals love starting a night out with a *pa amb oli* – bread with tomatoes, garlic and olive oil. This place is one of the most famous. *Plaça d'Artrutx 2 | ⊞ d6*

# AROUND CIUTADELLA

### ■ CALA SANTANDRIA

*5km south of Ciutadella / 12 mins (by car on the Me-24)*

This is where Menorca's relatively young tourist industry began. Bare rock, lots of buildings, hotels, bars, villas, restaurants – and not much greenery. The beach is white and a bit gritty. The entrance to the bay is guarded by an 18th-century British defence tower.

One unusual sight is the cave which Nicolau Cabrisas, the sculptor and local celebrity, used as a home and workshop. Over the years the artist covered his home and workshop with masks, grotesque faces and figurines. Since his death the cave has been closed to the public. However, the artist also designed the adjacent restaurant *Sa Nacra (Cala Santandria, on the northern shore of the bay | tel. 971 38 62 06 | €-€€)* built directly into the cliff. The terrace juts out over the azure sea.

**INSIDER TIP**
**Float above the sea**

Watching sunset here is very romantic with candlelight, great tapas and local wines. At lunchtime there is really delicious paella. But beware: in high season you will not get in without a reservation. If you want to go diving you should head to *Poseidon (C/ dels Suissos 3 | tel. 971 38 26 44 | tauch schule-poseidon-menorca.com)*, while at *Pedro's nightclub (C/ d'en Clates)* there is a firework display every night from May to September with laser shows and karaoke, flamenco and foam parties. *B4*

### 2 CALA BLANCA

*7km south of Ciutadella / 12 mins (by car on the Me-24)*

The name is shared by the holiday resort and the bay on its southern edge. The pristine white sand (hence the name) is offset by a backdrop of green pine forest. To the left and right of the beach the cliffs are covered with restaurants and bars, whose location is better than the food. A stunning sunset is pretty much guaranteed here on most evenings, for example from the beach bar *Hola Ola (Av. Llevant 11)*. *B4*

### 3 CALA EN BOSC

*11.5km south of Ciutadella / 26 mins (by car on the Me-24)*

Heading east from Cap d'Artrutx, the next resort is Cala en Bosc. The architecture here is pretty ugly, based more on functionality than aesthetics, but the beach on the edge of the resort makes up for it with its fine white sand and mostly clear waters. Informal *chiringuitos* (beach bars) will sell you food and drinks. A small tourist train on rubber wheels, the *minitren*, runs between Cap d'Artrutx and Son Xoriguer. The established water-sports school 👥 *Surf & Sail (on Son Xoriguer beach |mobile tel.*

Evening in Ciutadella

*629 74 99 44 | surfsailmenorca.com)* offers windsurfing and sailing courses *(from 40 euros/hr)* in summer. Kids will enjoy banana boat rides and stand-up paddling. *B5*

### 4 CALA PAREJALS

*14km south of Ciutadella / 28 mins (by car on the Me-24)*

This place is especially popular with Ciutadella's amateur anglers, and divers who like to catch and/or explore the rich and varied underwater world. Access is via a coastal path from *Platja de Son Xoriguer*. *B5*

## 5 CALA DE SON SAURA ☆ ☼

*15km southeast of Ciutadella / 32 mins (by car on the Camí de Son Saura)*

This bay is ideal for a day on the beach. It is sheltered from the wind and has two beaches, separated by a small spit of land, with beautiful white sand and shady pine trees. But beware: the cur-

is ochre coloured and there is shade here too. 🔲 C5

## 6 CALA EN TURQUETA ★ ☼

*14.5km southeast of Ciutadella / 29 mins (by car via Camí Cala en Turqueta)*

Along with Cala Macarella this pretty much defines what a good beach in

Take the plunge from a yacht into the Cala en Turqueta

rents in the bay can be strong. To get here from Ciutadella, take Camí de Sant Joan de Missa from the white church of the same name and turn off right at *Son Vivó* going past the old, square *Torre Saura Vell* tower. Road access to the beach is subject to a toll. Son Saura is popular with the people of Ciutadella so, if the long beach is already full, it is worth heading east. After crossing the rocky outcrop of *Punta d'es Governador* (approx. 500m) you come to the next, considerably smaller bay, *Cala d'es Talaier*. The sand

the south of Menorca means. Its name means "turquoise cove" and that is no exaggeration. Gently rounded cliffs protect a deep bay whose azure sea and white sands will tempt you to stay. To get there from Ciutadella, take the Camí de Sant Joan de Missa, bearing left at the junction in Son Vivó. After around 5km the road forks: left takes you to Cala Macarella, right to Cala en Turqueta. The car parks are often full at weekends. In the summer, boats (or the no. 68 bus) can drop you here saving you the stress of parking. 🔲 C5

## ⑦ CALA MACARELLA ★ ⚜

*17km southeast of Ciutadella / 30 mins (by bus and boat in the summer, otherwise by car via Camí de Macarella)*

This is Menorca's version of paradise: clear azure water, bordered by a ring of grey limestone, and behind the strip of sand a small wetland where turtles once lived. At the moment, only a bar hidden in the pine trees caters for beachgoers' needs with simple (and overpriced) dishes. In the cliffs along the shore there are some prehistoric caves. A footpath heads west to *Cala Macarelleta*, a nudist beach. The best way to experience this idyllic bay is on the water: try a *boat trip from Ciutadella* (see p. 101). Alternatively, take the 🚌 bus from Ciutadella (*July/Aug daily every 20 mins; June and 1–15 Sept daily every 40 mins | bus2macarella.com*). The return trip costs 8.40 euros and you'll have a more relaxed day. *Ⅲ D5*

## ⑧ SON CATLAR

*10.1km southeast of Ciutadella / 18 mins (by car via Camí de Son Saura)*

The largest prehistoric settlement area in the Balearics, Son Catlar is surrounded by a partly ruined wall. Inside there are cisterns, the foundations of living space, five stone towers *(talaiots)* and the central shrine, the *taula*. The age of the site is still unknown; all that is certain is that it was inhabited until the end of the Roman occupation. *Admission 3 euros | access via the path to the Platja de Son Saura | Ⅲ C4*

## ⑨ TORRE LLAFUDA

*11.7km east of Ciutadella / 17 mins (by car via the Ronda Nord and Me-1)*

**INSIDER TIP**
*Fairy-tale archaeology*

This large prehistoric settlement has a magical, almost eerie feel to it. It competes for space with a grove of holm oaks and there are well-preserved rooms, chambers, man-made caves, cisterns, a stone tower and a *taula*, all in the shade of the trees. *Access via the main Ciutadella–Maó road, Km37, then right after about 250m | Ⅲ C3-4*

## ⑩ NAU DES TUDONS ★

*7.8km east of Ciutadella / 16 mins (by car on Ronda Nord and Me-1)*

The island's best-known prehistoric grave and probably the oldest known building in Europe. The mighty sandstone blocks were assembled around 3,400 years ago. In the course of the excavation pieces of jewellery and the remains of human bones were found, suggesting that this was a (plundered) burial chamber. The interior of the *nau* (Spanish *naveta*) is divided in two floors.

There is a legend attached to the structure: two young giants are said to have argued about a woman. As proof of their love, one was to build a two-storey tower, the other to dig a well until he found water; the first to finish would win the woman's hand. The water flowed first and that so enraged the other giant that he picked up a huge stone from his tower (the current entrance hole) and threw it at the giant who had dug the well, killing him. The villain then drowned himself in the well and the woman died of a broken heart. The well is still known by the name *Pou de Sa Barrina* (Well of the Driller). *Admission 2 euros | Ctra Me-1 between Ciutadella and Ferreries, Km40 |▥ C3*

### ⑪ PEDRERES DE S'HOSTAL ☻

*5.5km east of Ciutadella / 10 mins (by car on the Ronda Nord/RC-1)*

Once a limestone quarry, today this is a semi-underground museum with stone mazes, "magical" gardens and huge rock sculptures. A great place to get lost! In the summer, concerts and dance shows are performed in front of the dramatic backdrop. *Nov–Feb daily 9.30am–2.30pm, Mar–Oct also Mon–Sat 4.30pm–sunset, Sun 9.30am–2.30pm | admission in winter free, otherwise 6 euros, children always free | Camí vell, Km1 | lithica.es |▥ C3*

> **INSIDER TIP**
> **A-maze-ing venue!**

### ⑫ PUNTA NATI

*6.3km north of Ciutadella / 12 mins (by car on the Cf-5)*

Sheep come here in search of the herbs that sprout between the craggy rocks. In spring the inhabitants of Ciutadella also take the bumpy road to Punta Nati. You'll have to travel the last few kilometres to the cape on foot but it's absolutely worth it. The promontory has been capped by a lighthouse since 1913. ☛ At night the area turns into a kind of open-air observatory – you can see the stars with amazing clarity as there is no light pollution. By day the view isn't

bad either – you look out over the sea and the rugged coastline towards two bays further east, *Cala es Pous* and *Cala es Morts*. This name, meaning "Bay of the Dead", refers to an incident which occurred in the winter of 1910 when a French ship steered into the cliffs and sank. Of the 150 people on board, only one young Frenchman survived the tragedy. A cross serves as a memorial to the accident. ▥ B2

### ⑬ CALA EN FORCAT

*6.2km west Ciutadella / 11 mins (by car on Ctra a Cala en Blanes)*

This resort is in the cliffs to the northwest of Ciutadella. The resorts of *Cala en Blanes*, *Cala en Forcat* and *Cala en*

*Brut* have become so enmeshed with the resort of *Los Delfines* that it is hard to see where one resort ends and another begins. Around them are luxury villas with incredible sea views. Each of the bays has at least one small beach. The largest is the one at *Cala en Blanes*, around 50m wide. However, you will look here in vain for wide, empty beaches – especially in summer. Kids will love the 🎡 *Aqua Center (May–Sept daily 10.30am–6.30pm | admission 20 euros, children 10 euros (under 3s free) | Cala en Blanes | Av. Principal, Urb. Los Delfines | aqua center-menorca.com)*, with its slides, "adventure river" and "black hole". 📖 *A3–4*

# CALA MORELL

📖 *C2* **Take some azure water, a semi-circular bay and white houses clinging to ruddy brown cliffs. Mix it all together and you get the resort of Cala Morell on the north-west coast!**

The architecture of the complex is reminiscent of Ibiza with some Menorcan elements, such as the imaginatively installed water outlets which lighten the austere appearance of many homes. The small beach here is normally fully of snorkellers admiring the fish.

The setting sun casts a golden light over Punta Nati

A great spot for snorkelling: Platja des Bots on Cala Algaiarens

## SIGHTSEEING

### CALA MORELL NECROPOLIS

Tourists are not the first people to love this bay. Menorca's first settlers used a small part of it to build a settlement into the rock thousands of years ago (around 900 BCE). The 70 artificial caves (some with supporting pillars and niches) are easily accessible from the road. With limestone higher up and red sandstone below, this is where the imaginary line begins which geologists use to divide Tramuntana in the north from Migjorn in the south. It extends all the way to Maó.

# AROUND CALA MORELL

### 14 CALA ALGAIARENS ✳🌴

*7.5km east of Cala Morell / 15 mins (by car via Camí de Cala Morell and Camí d'Algaiarens)*

This sheltered, semi-circular bay has two beaches, the Platja des Bots and the Platja es Tancats, and is one of few places on the north coast where the sea is calm enough to swim. The sand here comes in a broad palette of colours from white to reddish. The

water is crystal clear and you can always see the bottom, so it's ideal for snorkelling.

The eastern part of the bay is particularly pretty thanks to the freshwater lagoon that holds winter rainfall which has come down the *Barranc La Vall* before flowing into the sea here. ⅏ *C2*

### ▣ CAVALLS SON ÀNGEL ⚑

*4.2km southeast of Cala Morell / 7 mins (by car on the Camí de Cala Morell and Camí d'Algaiarens)*
This stud farm is a perfect stop for the horsily inclined. Its friendly staff run a range of guided hacks (also for beginners). There are one-hour tours of the finca up to four-hour treks along the coastal path. *From 20 euros/hr. | Camí d'Algaiarens "La Vall", Km1 | Toni Bosch: mobil tel. 649 48 80 98 | cavallssonangel.com | ⅏ C3*

# DISCOVERY TOURS

Want to get under the skin of the region? Then our discovery tours are the ideal guide – they provide advice on which sights to visit, tips on where to stop for that perfect holiday snap, a choice of the best places to eat and drink, and suggestions for fun activities.

## ① MENORCA AT A GLANCE

➤ Stylish ports in the old and new capitals
➤ Lagoons and bays with crystal-clear water
➤ Black and white lighthouses against the cliffs

📍 Binibèquer Vell     🏁 Cap d'Artrutx

→ 140km     🚗 2 days (3½ hrs total driving time)

ℹ️ Don't forget your swimming costume and adequate sun protection.
**❼ Alaior** has a big crafts market every Wednesday evening.
Avoid doing the second day's itinerary on a Monday because the bar/restaurant at the lighthouse, **Es Far d'Artrutx,** is closed.

Brightly coloured houses line the harbour promenade Moll de Llevant in Maó

## COFFEE IN A PIRATE'S LAIR

Start at ❶ Binibèquer Vell ➤ p. 59 with a Mediterranean breakfast of croissants and a steaming cup of *café amb llet* (milky coffee) at Cafetería Binibeca Vell *(daily | Carrer S'Ancora 1 | €€)*. This picture-perfect resort in the southeast of Menorca is a replica of a traditional pirates' cove. *From here it is about a 20-minute drive to* ❷ Maó ➤ p. 44 where you can get a good feel for the town by walking from the Plaça de S'Esplanada (car park) to the old town and from there down to the harbour. *To leave the town, head along the quieter Ronda de Sant Joan, which from the left joins the Me-7 main road to Fornells.* From here the landscape becomes gentler, greener and more tranquil and you will soon be driving through the island's nature reserves in the northeast.

## THE ISLAND'S RUGGED SIDE

*About halfway along the reserve, turn right onto the Cf-1 and head to the lighthouse at* ❸ Cap de Favàritx ➤ p. 72, which stands on weathered cliffs above the sea; it's a remote and rugged corner of the island. *Back on the Me-7 carry on to the small coastal resort of* ❹ Fornells ➤ p. 68. Perched on the banks of a large

**DAY 1**
❶ **Binibèquer Vell**

11.5km

❷ **Maó**

17km

❸ **Cap de Favàritx**

25km

❹ **Fornells**

saltwater lagoon, with fishing boats reflected in the tranquil waters, you can enjoy a cool drink at the Bar La Palma before moving on. Don't be tempted to get a snack because your lunch spot is not far away. *Head south on the Me-15 to* ❺ Es Mercadal ➤ p. 74, popular for its restaurants serving tasty, local food.

### MONASTIC TIPPLES & CRAFTY CRAFTS
After your meal the tour continues south, leaving the steppe landscape of the north coast behind to embrace pine groves which then in turn give way to the lush green pastures in the centre of the island. *On the eastern outskirts of Es Mercadel, a narrow tarmac road leads up to the barren* ❻ Monte Toro ➤ p. 75. After a few hairpin bends you reach its peak at 357m. From this, the highest point on Menorca, the view is fantastic. And, although you've just finished lunch in Es Mercadal, you should stop for a coffee or pastry at the monastic restaurant Sa Posada del Toro.

**INSIDER TIP**
**A feast for the eyes and the stomach**

There's always space for something sweet right? Or you could assist your digestion with one of their liqueurs. *A detour back towards Maó will take you to* ❼ Alaior

**9km**

❺ **Es Mercadal**

**4km**

❻ **Monte Toro**

**12km**

❼ **Alaior**

➤ p. 80, a traditional town famous for its arts and crafts and cheese-making. The Wednesday market (from 7pm onwards) is a good opportunity to check out local crafts and buy some of the delicious specialities. *Back on the road to Ciutadella, the Me-16 turns off to the right after about 3km to the sleepy resort of* ⑧ Es Migjorn Gran ➤ p. 85. After a splendid meal at the delightful guesthouse S'Engolidor *(closed Nov–April | C/ Major 3 | €€)* you can also spend the night here.

**EXPLORE THE OLD TOWN & JUMP INTO THE SEA**
Enjoy a decent breakfast before *continuing along the Me-20 down through the hairpin bends cut into reddish brown rock cliffs to Cala Galdana.* Schedule a break at ⑨ Ferreries ➤ p. 82 to take in the charm of the old part of town perched on the hill. *About 300m after leaving the resort, turn left onto the smaller Me-22 road.* After around 5km you will be treated to a wonderful view of the white sandy beaches and azure sea of ⑩ Cala Galdana ➤ p. 84. Take a refreshing plunge into the waves before enjoying a lunch at the restaurant El Mirador ➤ p. 84.

**FROM MASSIVE ROCKS TO CLIFF RESTAURANTS**
*Back on the Me-1, drive westwards and just before you reach the outskirts of Ciutadella, follow the road sign on your left* to one of the oldest buildings in Europe, the ⑪ Nau des Tudons ➤ p. 105 (a stop you should not miss). Wander among the enormous stones which appear to have been erected by giants. Now drive on to ⑫ Ciutadella ➤ p. 94, the west's main city. *Park near the Plaça de ses Palmeras (Alfonso III)* where you can start to explore this vibrant city: *stroll along the Carrer de Maó and Carrer de Josep Maria Quadrado and then down to Plaça d'es Born.* One of the

**INSIDER TIP**
**A pretty port**
prettiest bits of the whole city is the harbour, where restaurants are carved into the cliffs looking down on traditional llaut boats, yachts and passenger boats.

| | |
|---|---|
| 10.5km | |
| | ⑧ Es Migjorn Gran |
| **DAY 2** | |
| 6.5km | |
| | ⑨ Ferreries |
| 7.5km | |
| | ⑩ Cala Galdana |
| 21km | |
| | ⑪ Nau des Tudons |
| 4.5km | |
| | ⑫ Ciutadella |
| 12km | |

## COCKTAILS AT THE LIGHTHOUSE

*Drive south along the Me-24 until you reach the* spectacularly wild and rugged ⑬ Cap d'Artrutx with its lighthouse. How about a dip in the sea at the beautiful, tiny beach of Cala en Bosc, before joining in the evening ritual on the cape? The terrace of the light-house restaurant Es Far d'Artrutx *(closed Mon | Passeig Martítim | tel. 654 39 73 00 | €€)* is a great spot to watch the sunset: the rays of light transform the sea into vivid colours from yellow to saffron red. When the sun finally disappears, there is normally a round of applause.

⑬ Cap d'Artrutx

**INSIDER TIP**
**Lighthouse evenings**

# ❷ DARK CAVES & BLUE SEAS: WALK TO COVA DELS COLOMS

➤ Walk down through a green gorge
➤ Make a detour to a huge cave as big as a cathedral
➤ Round it off with a delicious meal on a dreamy beach

| | | | |
|---|---|---|---|
| 📍 | Es Migjorn Gran | 🏁 | Es Migjorn Gran |
| ↻ | 12.5km | 🚶 | ½ day (3 hrs total walking time) |
| ▁▃▅ | easy | ↗ | 140m |
| ℹ | Kit list: sturdy shoes, snacks, water, swimming stuff and a torch to explore the caves. Warning: ❶ Es Migjorn Gran is only served by buses from Ferreries and Maó in summer. | | |

## FROM THE LIMESTONE GORGE INTO THE GREEN

❶ Es Migjorn Gran

In ❶ Es Migjorn Gran ➤ p. 85, treat yourself to a fresh *ensaimada* and a coffee for breakfast at tapas bar La Palmera *(daily from 7am | C/ Major 83)* to fuel up for your walk. *Then drive through the resort heading south-west to the free car park near the cemetery. Take the*

1.5km

town's main road and turn left just before you leave the town into Cami de sa Malagraba. *After parking, walk along the Camí de Binigaus Nou, heading south.* The Binigaus Vell estate will come into view after 500m on the right where the road trails off and morphs into a path. *Follow the path to your left signposted "Cova dels Coloms". Continue along the footpath through fields and down into the limestone gorge,* the ❷ Barranc de Binigaus. The landscape changes abruptly and the eroded limestone gorge fills with greenery. Aleppo pines, olive trees and holly oaks tower upwards with great northern divers and hoopoes fluttering in their branches.

Gate to the underworld: Cova dels Coloms

## A "DOVES' CAVE" WITH A SACRED PAST

*Roughly halfway down to the sea, ignore the first left turn-off and, where the path forks after a short time, take the path straight on.* You will soon come to the wide, open mouth of the ❸ Cova dels Coloms ➤ p. 86 ("Doves' Cave"). The name relates to an ancient hunting custom: they used to stretch nets across the cave entrance to catch the doves nesting inside. Sacred objects from Menorcan prehistory have been found in the thick layer of clay on the cave floor, suggesting that the wide hall was once used for ritual activities. Take a moment to absorb the cathedral-like atmosphere.

## FOLLOW THE GORGE PATH TO THE BEACH

*Return to the main path at the bottom of the gorge and follow for a short distance. After five minutes you will reach a plateau where you take a path behind a gap in the wall heading back into the barranco. Turn left after 20m and then right up to the entrance of the* ❹ Cova de na Polida which is unfortunately closed to the

❷ Barranc de Binigaus

250m

❸ Cova dels Coloms

600m

❹ Cova de na Polida

2 km

public to protect a rare breed of bat which is living there. If the ban is ever lifted, make sure to look inside. *Having returned to the footpath, take the route down to the sea. When you reach a watering trough, take the signposted GR-223 path* where the gorge opens out into the **⑤ Platja de Binigaus** beach with its fine sand and azure sea, perfect for a dip. If you have forgotten to pack a picnic, you will find something to eat at **⑥ Urbanització Sant Tomàs**.

**⑤ Platja de Binigaus**
1km

**⑥ Urbanització Sant Tomàs**
7km

### SEAFOOD & FRUIT TREES

*Follow the beach eastwards to the beachside restaurant* Es Bruc ➤ p. 87. The fish tastes twice as good with a sea view (have it with some Menorcan wine). *To return to your car, walk to the end of the Platja de Binigaus and back along the same path to the watering trough. Then wander through the gorge until you reach the fork in the path after 10 minutes. Keep left and follow the cobblestone path uphill past wild fruit trees and through wild, romatic scenery. The path becomes wider, leading up to the Binigaus plain and back to the car park in* **① Es Migjorn Gran**.

> **INSIDER TIP**
> **Seafood and a sea breeze**

**① Es Migjorn Gran**

---

# ❸ CYCLE ALONG THE NORTHERN COAST

➤ Start off with a cheese tasting and a steep incline
➤ Beautiful views: the northern cape from a bird's perspective
➤ A walk on the cliffs and a refreshing dip at the "Horses' Beach"

| | | | |
|---|---|---|---|
| 📍 | Ferreries | 🏁 | Ferreries |
| 🔄 | 50km | 🚴 | 1 day (3 hrs/10km total walking time; 3½ hrs/40km total cycling time) |
| 📶 | very easy | ↗ | 100m |

ℹ Kit list: swimming stuff, sun hat, lots of water, comfortable shoes, picnic (if desired)
Caution: the first bit of the ride is very steep, take your time.
The hiking trail is the red GR-223.

### STOCK UP ON CHEESE FOR THE STEEP START

*This route starts on the eastern outskirts of* ❶ Ferreries ➤ p. 82, *to be precise at the petrol station in Polígono Industrial where you take the side road Camí de Sant Patrici and head north. A signpost points to the* ❷ Hort de Sant Patrici ➤ p. 85, *where you should take your first break.* This historic estate is not only surrounded by beautiful gardens, it also houses an attractive cheese museum. Stock up with a good portion of Queso de Maó … and maybe even try their wine because the next stretch will be hard work. *At the next fork in the road, keep right and head uphill (19 per cent gradient);* don't be disheartened, even experienced riders end up pushing here. Your hard work will soon be rewarded with fantastic views from the *Son Pere Nou estate* with the fjord-like Fornells bay to the north, pine-clad coasts to the south, the lagoon of S'Albufera des Grau to the east and green hills all around.

**INSIDER TIP**
**Cheesy treats**

❶ Ferreries

1.5km

❷ Hort de Sant Patrici

Holiday fun: cycling and hiking

## LIGHTHOUSE VISTAS

Before long the tarmac path comes to an end. *Take a sharp left towards the Sant Antoni's farmhouse. Then continue straight on. You'll soon pass through two gates, one iron, one wooden.* As you cycle along this route, Santa Águeda will be on your left, a 260-m mountain with the ruins of an Arabic fortress at the top. *Keep right at the next junction ignoring the entrance to the Son Rubí estate on your left. You will now join a tarmac path which takes you over a bridge to a crossroads where you can go left to Binimel·là beach, and right to Es Mercadal. You should continue straight on for a while until you reach the next large T-junction where you turn left. Continue along the tarmac known as Camí des Far ("Lighthouse Path") for a further 6km* – past the archaeological site at Ciutat Romana de Sanitja (currently not open to the public) – to the remote ❸ Cap de Cavalleria ➤ p. 70. Explore the area around the (closed off) lighthouse! The view to the east where it looks as if there's a sheer drop over the edge of the cliff is particularly spectacular.

**INSIDER TIP**
**Endless blue**

## A WALK ON THE IDYLLIC COAST PATH

*Return along the same road to a* ❹ parking spot *(approx. 4km away)* where you will see the signs for the start of the footpath. Lock up your bike and head off on foot towards the coast. You'll encounter one of the path's highlights at the very start of your walk: climb down the steps to the ❺ Platja de Cavalleria, a stunning double-crescent golden beach which is ideal for a dip! Then climb back up the steps and follow the picturesque coastal path to ❻ Cala Binimel·là ➤ p. 71. This red sandy beach is also a perfect location to enjoy a swim. If you have worked up an appetite, head to

16km

❸ Cap de Cavalleria

4km

❹ Parking spot

1km

❺ Platja de Cavalleria

3km

❻ Cala Binimel·là

2 km

Binimel·là restaurant *(closed Nov–April | tel. 971 35 92 75 |€–€€)*, which serves excellent Menorcan cuisine in the shade of fig trees. *Then follow the coastal path for another 20 minutes to* ❼ Cala Pregonda ➤ p. 71, with its bizarre rock formations. It's worth taking the same route back to the car park to enjoy the spectacular views.

## HOME COOKING & AMAZING VIEWS

Now it's time to get back on your bike and *cycle south-wards along the Camí des Far to the T-junction (approx. 3km) where you go left. After 1km, just before reaching Ses Cases Noves, your route takes you right along*

❼ Cala Pregonda

14km

another path through green plains. After 3km you'll reach another road which you follow left back to ❽ Es Mercadal ➤ p. 74. Take a well-earned break in this "culinary paradise" – there are plenty of restaurants to choose from – before one final push. *Now head west along the busy Me-1 for just 500m before turning right down the Camí d'en Kane.* This narrow romantic road, named after the British governor who ordered its construction in the 18th century, takes you past farmhouses in a picturesque hilly landscape. *After 6km it merges into the Me-1 which will bring you straight back to* ❶ Ferreries *(after about 2km).*

# ❹ UNSPOILED NATURE: A WALK IN ES GRAU

➤ Up and down: from one coastal pass to the next
➤ Any ospreys? Head along the lagoon's shore on wooden planks to get a look
➤ Have a proper picnic on the beach

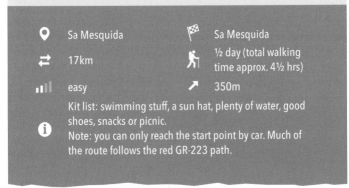

| | | | |
|---|---|---|---|
| 📍 | Sa Mesquida | 🏁 | Sa Mesquida |
| ⇄ | 17km | 🥾 | ½ day (total walking time approx. 4½ hrs) |
| 📶 | easy | ↗ | 350m |
| ℹ️ | Kit list: swimming stuff, a sun hat, plenty of water, good shoes, snacks or picnic. Note: you can only reach the start point by car. Much of the route follows the red GR-223 path. | | |

## THROUGH PASSES & BAYS TO THE LAGOON

Starting from the car park at ❶ Sa Mesquida ➤ p. 54, walk in the direction of the beach and keep left. At the end of the beach, the path leads up to the first pass and then descends to the neighbouring bay of ❷ Macar de Binillautí (*macar* is the term used in Menorca to

Start your walk at Sa Mesquida – if you can tear yourself away from the beach

describe a pebbly beach). *The path then ascends to a second pass and then down again to the bay of* ❸ Caleta de Binillautí. You pass through rugged scenery with bare rocks and barren steppe-like fields. *Shortly after leaving this bay, the path takes a turn inland, over another pass and through fields to the Me-5. Turn right and follow the road for 600m to the sign to Lagune S'Albufera. Cross the canal on the bridge and keep left at the next junction (signposted "Mirador").* Follow the wooden walkways, which protect the salt-loving plants underneath, down to the lagoon where you can often spot heron and even osprey.

| ❸ Caleta de Binillautí |
| --- |
| 3km |

## A SHADY PATH, PINE FOREST & DUNES

Head up a flight of steps to the viewpoint at ❹ Punta de sa Gola, with the vast lagoon now at your feet. The rolling hills head inland while the village of Es Grau is tucked into a far-off bay on the coast. *Climb down the steps and follow the walkway to the left.* The path leads you through a shady pine forest to the ❺ Platja d'Es Grau, dunes where you can bathe in the refreshing, turquoise waters.

| ❹ Punta de sa Gola |
| --- |
| 0.8km |

| ❺ Platja d'Es Grau |
| --- |
| 1.2km |

**SUNBATHE & SWIM**

*At the north end of the beach, the GR-223 signpost directs you inland through the pine forest.* En route you will pass another mirador offering a fantastic view of the black slate Cap de Favàritx and its lighthouse in the distance. The path then continues down to the ❻ Cala des Tamarells, a bay dominated by the old watchtower, Torre de Rambla. You can spend hours pretending you're stranded on this Robinson Crusoe beach – it is the ideal spot for sunbathing, a refreshing swim in the sea and a picnic.

❻ Cala des Tamarells

2.5km

**LISTEN TO THE WAVES LAP WHILE YOU FEAST**

*Follow the same route back to the Platja d'Es Grau and take a well-earned break in the village of* **7 Es Grau**  **➤ p. 73** *further south. Head for the terrace of* Bar Es Grau *(daily 9.30am–10pm | Plaça de Mestre Jaume 13 | €) for a light lunch of salad, a* bocadillo *("sandwich") or their dish of the day. From Es Grau follow the Me-5 road for around 1.5km until you hit the red-marked GR-223 on your left and can leave the tarmac behind you. You now go back over the three passes, accompanied by beautiful sea views all the way to* **1 Sa Mesquida**.

**7 Es Grau**

**6.5km**

**1 Sa Mesquida**

You'll spot the watchtower at Cala des Tamarells from far off

# GOOD TO KNOW

## HOLIDAY BASICS

# ARRIVAL

### GETTING THERE

Menorca is only about 2½ hours away from most UK airports. The best deals are those offered by charter flights, with or without a complete package, as well as part of special offers from the major tour organisers. But there are also good deals from scheduled carriers (most obviously the budget airlines). The Aeroport de Menorca (5km outside Maó) is well connected to most of the city by bus, but most tour operators have their own transfer networks between the airport and the hotels.

You can drive from the UK to Menorca but it involves crossing France and Spain on expensive motorways before finally taking the ferry from Barcelona and would take at least two whole days.

Ferries sail from Barcelona and València several times a week – more frequently in summer. Their destination is Port de Maó *(approx. 8 hrs)*. You can also use the cheap flights to neighbouring Mallorca and then take the Maó–Palma ferry *(6–7 hrs | Trasmediterránea-Acciona | Maó | Moll Comercial | tel. 902 45 46 45 | trasmediterranea.es)*. Another possible connection is Alcúdia–Ciutadella on the fast car ferry | *Baleària | tel. 902 16 0180 | balearia.com)*. Reservations are recommended in the summer season *(May–Oct)*, especially if you're travelling by car from the mainland.

### Adapter Type C

The mains voltage in all hotels and hostels is 230 volts. You will need a European adapter type C.

Ferries from mainland Spain and Mallorca dock at the Port de Maó

## GETTING IN

If arriving from a non-EU country, your passport needs to have been issued less than 10 years before the date you enter the country (check the "date of issue") and you must have at least 90 days on your passport after the day you plan to leave (check the "expiry date"). You will need to go through passport control. The queues can take a while.

## CLIMATE & WHEN TO GO

Most people come to Mallorca between mid-June and mid-September. It is particularly busy in July and August. The hotels and activity centres get booked up fast and even the more remote beaches can have queues of people waiting to park. If you can, come in spring (April/May) or autumn (October) – this is when Menorca is at its best, with great weather but not too many tourists. In winter (November to

March) when the weather is cool and windy, very few tourists come to the island.

# GETTING AROUND

## BIKE

You can hire bicycles in virtually every resort but motorbikes are only available in Ciutadella und Maó. *Bike Menorca* in *Maó (Av. Francesc Femenías 44 | bikemenorca.com)* hires out all kinds of bikes from racers to moutain bikes and *Velos Joan (velos joan.com)* is a good option, with branches in both cities.

## BUS

The public transport network is run by three companies: *TMSA (tel. 971 36*

04 75 | *tmsa.es), Autos Fornells (mobile tel. 686 93 92 46 | auto fornells.com)* and *Torres (tel. 971 38 64 61 | bus.e-torres.net).* The network and the current bus timetables can be viewed at *menorca.tib.org*.

## CAR

You can hire a car at the airport and in all the major tourist resorts. The cheapest provider on the island is *Tramuntana (tel. 650 65 70 45 | tramuntanarentacar.es)*, where you can get a rental car for a week from 15 euros per day (a car for one day costs from 35 euros). The service is unbeatable as well: the car will be delivered to any village on the island without a surcharge; you don't have to pay extra for a second driver, and there are no tricks when filling up the tank.

**INSIDER TIP**
**As honest as they come**

Diesel and unleaded *(sin plomo)* petrol can be purchased from 11 petrol stations on the island: in Maó, Ciutadella, Alaior, Sant Lluís, Es Mercadal and on the road between Maó and Fornells.

## TAXI

You can find taxis even in the smaller towns, usually at a designated taxi rank. Prices start at 3 euros and each kilometre costs 2 euros more. Should there be no taxi waiting, call a company. *Maó: tel. 971 36 71 11 | Ciutadella: tel. 971 48 2222 taxismenorca.com*

## HIGHWAY CODE

In built up areas the speed limit depends on the size of road, narrow single-lane streets are limited to 20kmh; if there is one lane in each direction it is 30kmh; and where there are more than one lane in each direction it is 50kmh.

On rural roads, the limit is 80kmh, but if there is a hard shoulder at least 1.5m wide, then it's 100kmh. Seatbelts are obligatory for both front and back-seat passengers (if belts are fitted in the rear). Wearing a helmet is obligatory for moped and motorbike riders. Motorists must carry two reflective vests and two warning triangles in case of accident or breakdown; the use of a mobile phone without hands-free facility is strictly prohibited. And breathalyser tests are carried out frequently; the drink-drive limit is 0.5g of blood alcohol per litre.

# FESTIVALS & EVENTS
## ALL YEAR ROUND

### MARCH/APRIL
**Setmana Santa (Holy Week):** On Good Friday and Easter Sunday choirs perform all over the island.

### MAY
**8 May, Festa de la Verge del Toro** (Monte Toro): The island's patron saint is venerated atop the highest mountain.

### JUNE
**Diumenge des Be** (across the island): "Sunday of Sheep" launches the St John celebrations with a procession of sheep through the streets.

**23/24 June, ★ Festes de Sant Joan** (Ciutadella): Highlight of the festival week with cavalcades *(caragols)*, concerts and fireworks.

**29 June, Festa de Sant Pere** (Maó): Fishing festival with regattas.

### JULY
**15/16 July, Festa del Carme** (Maó, Ciutadella, Fornells): Boat processions.

**24/25 July, Festa de Sant Jaume** (Es Castell): Equestrian shows, music and fireworks.

**3rd Sun of July, Festa de Sant Martí**: In honour of St Martin with processions and parades.

### JULY/AUGUST
**End July-end Aug, Matins de l'orgue** *(*Maó): Free organ recitals at Santa María as well as the **Festival de Música de Maó** *(festivalde musicademao.com)*.

**9 Aug-beginning Sept, Festival de Música d'Estiu** (Ciutadella): Festival with musicians and artists; some events are held at the former quarry *L'Hostal de Líthica* (pedravivamenorca.com).

**3rd weekend Aug, Festes de Sant Climent** (Sant Climent): Water fights and equestrian shows.

### SEPTEMBER
**7-9 Sept, ⚑ Festes de la Verge de Gràcia** (Maó): Processions, equestrian displays, religious services and fireworks to honour Maó's patron saint.

**Festival de Jazz** (Maó and Ciutadella): Featuring international stars.

# EMERGENCIES

## CONSULATES & EMBASSIES
### UK HONORARY VICE CONSULATE
*Cami Biniatap 30 | Horizonte | tel. +34 902 109 356 | Mon–Fri 10am–midday*

### US CONSULATE
There is no consulate on Menorca, but there is one on Mallorca: *c/Porto Pi, 8–9D | Palma de Mallorca | tel. +34 971 40 37 07 | Mon–Fri 10.30am–1.30pm | es.usembassy.gov/consular-agency-palma-de-mallorca*

## EMERGENCY SERVICES
Call 112 – for the police, fire brigade and ambulance. This service is also available in English.

If you lose your bank or credit card, contact your bank in the UK immediately and report the theft to the police. Make sure you have made a note of your card company's 24-hour contact phone number before you go away. If your cards are registered with a card protection agency, ensure you have their contact number and your policy number with you.

## HEALTH
Chemists *(farmacias)* are indicated with a green cross. When closed, a notice will inform you of the nearest emergency chemist.

Make sure you have comprehensive travel or health insurance in case of emergencies. Medical services often have to be paid for at the point of use, in which case it is important to get a receipt *(recibo oficial)* from the doctor (also for expensive medicines or dental treatment) so that you can be reimbursed.

In the holiday resorts there are special *centros médicos* which are equipped to deal with medical needs, communication problems and the most common holiday illnesses. Dentists are listed under *dentista*. You can call for an ambulance day and night on *tel. 061*.

# ESSENTIALS

## ACCOMMODATION
type of accommodation imaginable is available on Menorca from five-star hotels to basic B&Bs, holiday lets and *fincas*, which are a popular option. Most of the bigger hotels are on the western and southern coasts but Maó and Ciutadella also have plenty to choose from.

## BEACHES
There are more than 80 beaches along the 216km of coastline in Menorca. The biggest are in the south but the north has lots of charming spots too. Services such as lifeguards, toilets and showers are only found in larger resorts. In contrast to the other Balearic islands, Menorca has no designated nudist beaches. But topless bathing is tolerated on all beaches and in small, hidden-away bays people also sunbathe in the nude.

Even if the water looks calm be very aware of the currents (especially on the bigger beaches) and look out for warning flags/buoys. All the important information on Menorca's beaches can be found at *platges debalears.com* and *menorca.es*. Beaches with lifeguards display flags to indicate the status of the water. Green means swimming is definitely ok, yellow means it is dangerous, and red means it is forbidden.

## CAMPING

To find out whether or not camping is allowed, you need to check with the local council or the property owner. Wild camping is generally inadvisable and is banned in all conservation areas. There are two campsites: *S'Atalaia (May–Oct | Ferreries–Cala Galdana, Km4 | tel. 971 37 42 32 | campingsatalaia.com)*, in a pine forest 3km from the coast; and *Son Bou (April–Oct | Ctra de San Jaume, Km3.5 | tel. 971 37 27 27 | campingsonbou. com)*, which has lots of sports facilities.

## CUSTOMS

If travelling within the EU, there are very few strict customs rules. However, if travelling from outside the EU you will need to check your allowances before bringing things in or out of the country.

## INFORMATION

The two main tourist information office in *Maó (Oficina de Información Turística | Plaça Constitució 22 | tel. 971 35 59 52)* and *Ciutadella (Plaça d'es Born 15 | tel. 971 48 41 55)* can answer most questions. There is also an info stand at the airport *(arrivals*

*hall | summer only)* and at *Maó's port (Moll de Llevant 2 | tel. 971 35 59 52)*, as well as a mobile tourist info kiosk which moves around the major resorts.

## LANGUAGE

You can get by quite well on Menorca with English, but Spanish *(castellano)* is, of course, even better. If you'd like to surprise your host with a few words in *català*, you will find a few expressions in "Useful words and phrases", p. 132. But remember that there are some differences between the *menorquí* dialect and "mainland" Catalan.

## MONEY

Banks are usually only open 9am–1pm or 2pm. There are numerous ATMs and credit cards are widely used and are accepted in almost all shops, hotels and restaurants. Card providers

### HOW MUCH DOES IT COST?

| | |
|---|---|
| Coffee | from 1.50 euros for a latte |
| Snack | from 2 euros for a tapa |
| Daily menu | from 10 euros for a menú del día |
| Abarques | 15-30 euros for a pair of typical Menorcan sandals |
| Fuel | 1.40-170 euros for 1 litre of Eurosuper |
| Nightclub | 15-25 euros admission in the evening |

with the most extensive network on the island are VISA, Mastercard and Eurocard; American Express and Diners Club are not as widely accepted.

## NATIONAL HOLIDAYS

| | |
|---|---|
| **1 Jan** | Cap d'any, New Year |
| **6 Jan** | Tres Reis, Epiphany |
| **17 Jan** | Festa de Sant Antoni, Saint Anthony |
| **1 March** | Dia de les Illes Balears, Balearics Day |
| **March/April** | Maundy Thursday; Good Friday |
| **1 May** | Festa de Treball, Labour Day |
| **15 Aug** | L'Assumpció, Feast of Assumption |
| **12 Oct** | Dia de l'Hispanitat, Discovery of America |
| **1 Nov** | Tots Sants, All Saints' Day |
| **6 Dec** | Dia de la Constitució, Constitution Day |
| **8 Dec** | La Immaculada Concepció, Immaculate Conception |
| **25/26 Dec** | Nadal, Christmas |

## OPENING TIMES

Normally, shops are open Mon–Fri 9am–1.30pm and 5–8pm, on Saturdays it's morning only. In peak season (mid-May–Feb), most restaurants are open daily, from midday to 10 or 11 in the evening. (Opening times in this guide refer to peak season, if not otherwise stated.) In the off-season, many hotels are closed and many restaurants are not open daily, so you should check current opening times beforehand on the restaurant's website.

## POST

Postage for letters and postcards within Europe is currently 1.45 euros. You can buy stamps at the post office and in all the tobacconists identified with the national colours; post offices are only open in the mornings (in Maó all day). The main post offices are: *Alaior (C/ Forn 1); Ciutadella (Pl. des Born 5); Es Castell (C/ Llevant); Maó (C/ Bonaire 15).*

## PRICES

Prices on Menorca are a little higher than they are on the mainland, especially for certain food items. The admission fee for museums is between 3 and 6 euros, the set menu in an average restaurant costs 15–30 euros.

An accommodation tax is slapped on the hotel price in peak season (May–Oct) per night per guest over 16. It is meant to help with nature protection. The amount (2-4 euros) depends on the hotel category. Reductions are available for students and pensioners.

## TELEPHONE & WIFI

The international dialling code for Spain is +34, followed by the 9-digit number. For the UK it's +44 and for the US and Canada +1.

Your mobile phone can be used without any problems although some phone companies are currently reintroducing roaming fees, so check and be aware of your usage.

The island's government has launched a free 30-minute WiFi service accessible in all larger resorts. Most cafés, restaurants and hotels (nearly always in the reception area) have also set up small WiFi zones. Visitors generally have to ask at the reception or the restaurant owner for the access code: "Cuál es la clave de la

red inalámbrica?" You will be charged for use more frequently here than on the Spanish mainland (3–6 euros a day). Your travel operator or concierge can provide more information.

**TIPPING**

As a rule, 5–10 per cent of the bill is appropriate for restaurant waters. Chamber maids, porters, taxi drivers and guides should all get a tip.

## WEATHER IN MAÓ

High season
Low season

| | JAN | FEB | MARCH | APRIL | MAY | JUNE | JULY | AUG | SEPT | OCT | NOV | DEC |
|---|---|---|---|---|---|---|---|---|---|---|---|---|
| Daytime temperature | | | | | | | | | | | | |
| | 14° | 14° | 16° | 18° | 21° | 25° | 28° | 28° | 26° | 22° | 18° | 14° |
| Night-time temperatures | | | | | | | | | | | | |
| | 7° | 7° | 9° | 11° | 13° | 17° | 20° | 20° | 19° | 15° | 11° | 9° |
| ☀ | 5 | 5 | 6 | 8 | 10 | 10 | 12 | 10 | 8 | 6 | 5 | 4 |
| 🌧 | 9 | 8 | 8 | 7 | 5 | 3 | 1 | 3 | 6 | 11 | 9 | 12 |
| ≈ | 14 | 13 | 14 | 14 | 17 | 20 | 23 | 25 | 23 | 21 | 18 | 15 |

☀ Hours of sunshine per day    🌧 Rainy days per month    ≈ Sea temperature in °C

# USEFUL PHRASES
## CATALAN

## SMALL TALK

| | |
|---|---|
| Yes/no/maybe | sí/no/potser |
| Please | sisplau |
| Thank you | gràcies |
| Hi/Hello/Good evening/Goodnight! | Hola!/Bon dia!/Bona tarda!/ Bona nit! |
| Goodbye | Adéu! Passi-ho bé! |
| My name is | Em dic ... |
| What is your name? (formal); What is your name? (informal) | Com es diu?/Com et dius? |
| I come from | Sóc de ... |
| Excuse me (informal/formal) | Perdona!/Perdoni! |
| Please could you repeat? (formal/ informal) | Com diu?/Com dius? |
| I (don't) like this | (No) m'agrada. |
| I would like ... / Do you have ...? | Voldria .../Té ...? |
| May I ...? | Puc ...? |

## SYMBOLS

## EATING & DRINKING

| | |
|---|---|
| Could I please have …? | **Podria portar-me …?** |
| knife/fork/spoon | **ganivet/forquilla/cullera** |
| salt/pepper/sugar | **sal/pebrot/sucre** |
| vinegar/oil | **vinagre/oli** |
| milk/cream/lemon | **llet/crema de llet/llimona** |
| with/without ice, fizzy/still | **amb/sense gel/gas** |
| cold/too salty/too rare | **fred/salat/cru** |
| Could we get the bill, please? | **El compte, sisplau.** |
| bill/receipt | **compte/rebut** |
| tip | **propina** |
| cash/credit card | **al comptat/amb targeta de crèdit** |

## MISCELLANEOUS

| | |
|---|---|
| Where is/are …? | **On està …?/On estan …?** |
| What time is it? | **Quina hora és?** |
| How much does … cost? | **avui/demà/ahir** |
| Where can I find somewhere with internet/Wifi? | **Quant val …?** |
| Can I take a photo of you/here? | **On em puc connectar a Internet/ WLAN?** |
| Help!/Watch out! | **Puc fer-li una foto aquí?** |
| broken | **Ajuda!/Compte!** |
| breakdown/garage | **trencat** |
| pharmacy/drugstore | **avaria/taller** |
| fever/pain | **farmàcia/drogueria** |
| timetable/ticket | **febre/dolor** |
| ban/banned | **horario/bitllet** |
| open/closed | **prohibició/prohibit** |
| right/left/straight on | **obert/tancat** |
| more/less | **a la dreta/a l'esquerra/tot recte** |
| cheap/expensive | **més/menys** |
| (not) drinking water | **barat/car** |
| (kein) Trinkwasser | **aigua (no) potable** |
| 0/1/2/3/4/5/6/7/8/9/10/100/1000 | **zero/un, una/dos, dues/tres/ quatre/cinc/sis/set/vuit/nou/deu/ cent/mil** |

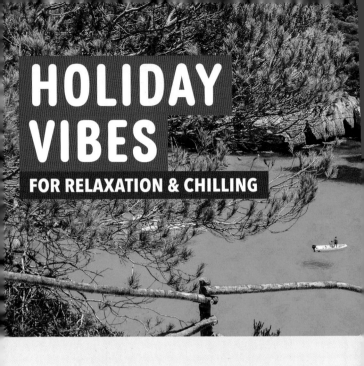

# HOLIDAY VIBES
## FOR RELAXATION & CHILLING

## FOR BOOKWORMS & FILM BUFFS

### 📖 A BOOK OF DAYS

It is on Menorca that the 533 days of writing take place. Dutch poet and novelist Cees Noteboom explores his immediate surroundings and his love for Menorca as well as more general observations on life (2021).

### 📖 THE VACATIONERS

There are disappointingly few books set on Menorca, but Emma Straub's tale of a holiday that goes wrong on the neighbouring island of Mallorca is a wonderful Balearic beach read (2014).

### 📖 WALK! MENORCA

David and Ros Brawn have written a comprehensive guide to walks in Menorca with ratings for distance, time etc. There are clear maps and photos. But buy it before you go because it is not available in Menorca (2005).

### 🎥 ISLA BONITA

A love letter to the island and its culture. Fernando Colomo's light 2016 comedy was filmed on Menorca and tells the story of a director going through a mid-life crisis. The Menorcan backdrop is amazing – bright sunlight, crystal-clear water and enchanting flora (2016).

# PLAYLIST

0:58

**❚❚ LEONMANSO – SET MIL DOS-CENTS**
A son of Ciutadella pays tribute to his hometown in a poetic and unusual way.

**▶ JOANA PONS AMB SES GUITARRES** – XOROI
Menorcan folk music borrows from many cultural traditions. This is a melancholic song about the pirate *Xoroi*.

**▶ LALO GARAU** – DE LA MAR
Mallorcan musician Lalo Garau sings about the Balearic sea.

**▶ BANDA DE FERRERIES** – NURA I ELS TITANS DE LA PEDRA
A composition inspired by Menorca's *talaiots*.

**▶ ISMAEL PONS-TENA – MARAVILLA**
This well-known baritone from Maó loves to sing *zarzuelas* (Spanish operettas).

The holiday soundtrack is available at **Spotify** under **MARCO POLO** Menorca

Or scan the code with the Spotify app

## ONLINE

**ELPALADAR.ES**
You can order Menorcan specialities such as wine or cheese online on this website.

**GOBMENORCA.COM**
The website of the Balearic ornithological association which has a blog. It is highly informative even if the English translation is a bit idiosyncratic.

**CAMÍ DE CAVALLS**
An app to help you explore the island's best hiking trails and footpaths (including the "Horse Path" in its title).

**SHORT.TRAVEL/MEN4**
Do you want to spend some time exploring Menorca's underwater world? This video will get you in the mood for diving adventures.

**SHORT.TRAVEL/MEN3**
Another video to inspire you. This bird's eye view of Menorca will give you a great idea of the island's beauty, although the commentary is in Spanish only.

# TRAVEL PURSUIT

## THE MARCO POLO HOLIDAY QUIZ

Do you know your facts about Menorca? Here you can test your knowledge of the little secrets and idiosyncrasies of the island and its people. You will find the correct answers below, with further details on pages 20 to 25 of this guide.

**❶** Where does the recipe for mayonnaise come from?
a) Menorca's capital, Maó
b) Cala Morell
c) Es Mercadal

**❷** How many kilometres of stone wall are there on Menorca?
a) 1,000km
b) 10,000km
c) 20,000km

**❸** What language do Menorcans speak?
a) Castilian Spanish
b) Català
c) Menorquí

**❹** Why do so many place names begin with the prefix "Bini"?
a) Because *bini* comes from *bene* and there are so many beautiful places on Menorca
b) Because in Arabic *bini* means "property of the sons of"
c) Because it was the name of Alfonso III's wife

**❺** Which bird species is particularly at home on Menorca?
a) Heron
b) Scopoli shearwater
c) Flamingo

Correct answers: 1a, 2c, 3c, 4b, 5b, 6c, 7b, 8a, 9a, 10a

Stone walls are a characteristic feature of the Menorcan landscape

**❻ How many ancient *talaiot* sites are there on Menorca?**
a) 16
b) 160
c) 1,600

**❼ What are *barrancs* and why are there so many on Menorca?**
a) Predatory fish – they find a lot to eat in the sea around Menorca
b) Deep gorges – hewn out of the limestone by rain
c) Gently rolling hills – formed by centuries of winemaking

**❽ Why are large ancient monumental constructions call *navetas* ("ships")?**
a) Because they look like the hull of a ship
b) Because they were probably used as shipyards
c) Because they are near the coast

**❾ What was Es Castell's first name?**
a) Georgetown
b) Saint George
c) Castellum

**❿ What is the most famous remnant of British rule on Menorca?**
a) Gin
b) Sash windows
c) Jersey cattle

# INDEX

## WE WANT TO HEAR FROM YOU!

Did you have a great holiday? Is there something on your mind? Whatever it is, let us know! Whether you want to praise the guide, alert us to errors or give us a personal tip – MARCO POLO would be pleased to hear from you.
Please contact us by email:

**sales@heartwoodpublishing.co.uk**

We do everything we can to provide the very latest information for your trip. Nevertheless, despite all of our authors' thorough research, errors can creep in. MARCO POLO does not accept any liability for this.

### PICTURE CREDITS

**Cover photo:** Cala Macarelleta (Schapowalow: R. Schmid)
**Photos:** I. Gawin (139); huber-images: D. Erbetta (rear inside cover flap, 14/15, 26/27, 45, 69, 97), M. Ripani (121), R. Schmid (16/17, 46, 56, 64/65, 76/77, 84, 90/91, 100, 136/137), Laif: M. Amme (34/35, 104), G. Azumendi (2/3, 89), Knechtel (13), T. Linkel (10, 30); Laif/Le Figaro Magazine: Martin (118); Laif/REA: F. Perri (25); Look: K. Maeritz (110/111); Look/age fotostock (11, 40/41, 72, 81, 95); Look/travelstock44 (22); K. Maeritz (98); mauritius images: S. Beuthan (83, 127), J. Warburton-Lee (61); mauritius images/age fotostock: (28/29, 52, 115), A. Leiva (8/9), M. Mayol (36/37); mauritius images/Alamy (32/33, 33, 48, 55, 86/87); mauritius images/Axiom Photographic (103); mauritius images/hemis.fr: R. Mattes (6/7); mauritius images/imagebroker: Stella (75); mauritius images/robertharding (62); mauritius images/Westend61 (12, 21); Shutterstock: C. Felderer (51), P. Kazmierczak (124/125, 134/135), K. Krivorotova (123), lunamarina (58, 107), Mariontxa (29), nito (front cover flap, front inside cover flap), Rulan (70), tuulijumala (108)

### 4th Edition – fully revised and updated 2023
**Worldwide Distribution:** Heartwood Publishing Ltd, Bath, United Kingdom
www.heartwoodpublishing.co.uk

**Authors:** Jörg Dörpinghaus, Izabella Gawin
**Editor:** Karin Liebe
**Picture editor:** Anja Schlatterer
**Cartography:** © MAIRDUMONT, Ostfildern (pp. 38–39, 112, 116, 119, 122, pull-out map; © MAIRDUMONT, Ostfildern, using data from OpenStreetMap, licence CC-BY-SA 2.0 (pp. 42–43, 44, 66–67, 78–79, 92–93, 96)
**Cover design and pull-out map cover design:** bilekjaeger_Kreativagentur mit Zukunftswerkstatt, Stuttgart
**Page design:** Lucia Rojas

**Heartwood Publishing credits:**
**Translated from the German** by John Owen, John Sykes, Susan Jones and Suzanne Kirkbright
**Editors:** Felicity Laughton, Kate Michell, Sophie Blacksell Jones
**Prepress:** Summerlane Books, Bath
**Printed** in India

MARCO POLO AUTHOR
### IZABELLA GAWIN

Izabella Gawin loves Spanish islands and has made a career writing about them. Menorca is her favourite of the Balearics: it's not as crowded as its neighbours and it has a fantastically varied coastline, with colours, shapes and sounds to beguile the senses.

# DOS & DON'TS

## HOW TO AVOID SLIP-UPS & BLUNDERS

### DON'T GET RIPPED OFF FOR WIFI
Hotels always offer internet but some will charge you 3-6 euros a day. There is plenty of free WiFi on Menorca, so don't get ripped off with absurd hotel rates.

### DON'T IGNORE JELLYFISH
The Portuguese man-of-war is especially nasty, with its burning sting and electric shocks. Please pay attention to the flags on the beach: if you see one with a medusa-head on it, stay out of the water. Washed up jellyfish are also a good sign that it is better to enjoy the beach than the water.

### DON'T CLIMB OVER WALLS
Make sure you respect Menorcans' property: always stick to marked paths and make sure you close gates behind you when walking in the countryside.

### DON'T GO TO TOWN ON SUNDAY
On Sundays there's nothing going on in Ciutadella or Maó, because that's when the locals go to the beach and tourist sights and shops are closed. If you want to experience the Mediterranean way of life, come back another day.